Remodelista
THE LOW-IMPACT HOME

Remodelista
THE LOW-IMPACT HOME

A Sourcebook for Stylish,
Eco-Conscious Living

Margot Guralnick & Fan Winston

With the editors of Remodelista
Principal photography by Matthew Williams

ARTISAN | NEW YORK

Contents

Introduction

Can style and sustainability coexist? It's a question we explore daily at Remodelista, the home design website we launched in 2007 with the aim of simplifying the remodeling process and celebrating the well made and the well designed. Since then, we've championed projects and products, with an eye toward not-too-muchness and a respect for the environment. We're a small group of design-obsessed writers, editors, and friends, and, like you, we feel the urgent need to respond to climate change. Which is why, now more than ever, we are embracing the idea of low-impact living.

What exactly does "low impact" mean? We like to think of it as the new normal: a personalized (if admittedly not perfect) future-minded approach to domestic life, with an emphasis on conscientious consumerism and responsible choices. In this book, we visit the living quarters of people who have interpreted this ethos in myriad ways. Among the projects featured: an Australian couple's compact net-zero house, a rental apartment in Brooklyn built with materials salvaged from the neighborhood, and a farmhouse in England made of hemp.

Can these choices move the needle? Yes, if you believe, as we do, that leading by example—and altering mindsets—is one way to get to much-needed collective change. So is learning from the wisdom of others: throughout the book, you'll find expert tips on how to greenify your life, from a gentler laundry routine courtesy of the sisters behind Brooklyn's hippest laundromat to chef David Tanis's low-tech approach to the kitchen artillery. Of course, we've included remodeling advice for all occasions, whether you're looking to source nontoxic paint, add a new rug, upgrade your windows, or overhaul your whole place.

You'll also discover plenty of our own favorite household essentials, plastic-free and planet friendly. Finally, we've rounded up Remodelista editors' favorite everyday heirlooms, all widely available secondhand. We hope you find inspiration in these pages: big and small steps to take, new practices to adopt, and a sense that an eco-conscious approach can and should be about living not only thoughtfully but also with joie de vivre and style.

The Low-Impact Manifesto

It's imperative to make choices at home that are healthy for ourselves and our planet. But we also have to get comfortable. Here are our ten essential tenets of living well while treading lightly.

1. **Make use of what you have.** Or, as the Depression-era motto goes, "Use it up, wear it out, make do, or do without."

2. **Fix it first.** Chances are, you have the tools to repair your moth-eaten sweater, broken coffeemaker, flickering lamp, or wobbly table—or know someone who does.

3. **Prioritize the secondhand.** Keeping things in circulation is the most impactful way to recycle. So before investing in something new, browse the vast world of used goods. Furniture and household essentials from the past are often better made and will give you more satisfaction than cheaply produced stand-ins. (See page 240 for a list of our 75 everyday favorites.)

4. **Borrow instead of buy.** Rather than acquiring goods that will end up hogging your precious storage space, share resources: join a "library of things" (see page 329) and check out tools and equipment of all sorts.

5. Don't succumb to trends. Seek artisan-made wares that you can share with the next generation. Support small, local businesses and make mindful purchases: the goal is to acquire something once and keep it for the long haul.

6. Avoid plastic. Commit to using household goods made of natural, long-lasting, biodegradable materials.

7. Adopt a "garbage is costly" mindset. If we all had to pay per bag to have our trash hauled away, we'd generate a lot less. Repurpose or compost what you can and, if need be, recycle the rest.

8. Grow your own. Minimize your carbon "foodprint" by tending a vegetable patch, fruit trees, even just a few windowsill pots of herbs. Nurturing plants elevates the spirit—and teaches us not only about the interconnectedness of everything but also why it's so essential to be in alliance with nature.

9. Embrace wabi-sabi. We're not perfect; why must our homes be? Learn to live with, and even appreciate, your creaky wood floors and too-small kitchen as they are. The same goes for the outdoors: instead of keeping a pristine, chemical-laden lawn, rewild your landscape and let Mother Nature take the wheel.

10. Live stylishly with less. Edit out what you don't need— pass down, donate, tag as "Free." You'll feel unencumbered, and what you use and love will take on the importance it deserves.

7 Easy Habit Shifts

1. Finish what's on your plate—and in your fridge. Food is the single biggest source of global carbon dioxide emissions, and an alarming percent of those emissions stem from food waste. Buy reasonable quantities—local, seasonal, plant-based ingredients are the ideal— and use what you've got, then compost your scraps (see page 181).

2. Heat the person, not the house. Install a smart thermostat, and lower your energy use when no one's home. In the winter, bundle up instead of blasting the heat. Similarly, use old-fashioned techniques to stay cool: install awnings and window blinds, position a fan to make the most of a cross breeze, take a quick cold shower, sleep on the porch.

3. Conserve water. Launder only what's really dirty. Instead of washing each dish under the tap, fill the sink or a bin with soapy water. Turn off the faucet while brushing your teeth and the shower while lathering up (leaving them on wastes thousands of gallons/liters of water per person per year). Collect shower water to use on your plants— and take an occasional sponge bath instead of a daily shower.

4. Say no to waste. Avoid buying products that come in single-use plastic and other unnecessary packaging, cancel catalogs (catalogchoice.org makes this easy and free), opt out of junk mail (to stop the barrage of credit card preapprovals, visit optoutprescreen.com), bypass flyers and business cards, and carry your own grocery and produce bags, as well as utensils and coffee cup.

5. Learn the recycling guidelines in your location and follow them. Adding questionable items to the heap is likely to contaminate the whole collection and make it nonrecyclable. (For details, see "Recycling 101," page 180.)

6. Use rags instead of paper towels and cloth napkins instead of paper ones. Old T-shirts are ideal cleaning cloths, and you can easily make your own napkins by cutting squares of scrap fabric (hems are nice but not essential). Big family? Give each person their own pattern or color, and add fresh napkins only as needed.

7. Replace your remaining incandescent lightbulbs with LEDs. They require a fraction of the energy and last so much longer (for more on LEDs, see page 228).

EXTRA CREDIT: 5 IMPORTANT, NOT-SO-EASY CHANGES

---

1. MAKE YOUR HOME AS ENERGY-EFFICIENT AS POSSIBLE AND USE GREEN ENERGY TO POWER IT.
Install solar panels on your roof, a heat pump in your basement, and an electric stove in your kitchen—the idea is to say no to fossil fuels. (For a deeper dive into this topic, see "The Inner Workings," page 294.)

2. EAT A PLANT-BASED DIET—OR, AT THE VERY LEAST, A LOT LESS MEAT.
Consider cutting down on dairy, too, and giving up beef, the most carbon-intensive of all foods.

3. GET AROUND ON PUBLIC TRANSPORT, BY BIKE, OR ON FOOT.
If having a car is crucial, it should be electric.

4. TRAVEL BY PLANE INFREQUENTLY, IF AT ALL.
The UN predicts CO_2 emissions from planes will triple by 2050. Consider getting to your destination by train instead.

5. FIND WAYS YOU, AS AN INDIVIDUAL, CAN HELP TIP THE SCALES.
Run for public office, start a community garden, launch a composting co-op, join (and lend financial support to) environmental action groups, and hold your legislators accountable. Use your skills and convictions to rally others.

12 LOW-IMPACT HOUSES AND GARDENS

Go net-zero? Install solar panels? Downsize? Recycle? Upcycle? Bicycle? Fortunately, there are countless ways, both big and small, to design a life and a home that are kinder to our planet. Let the examples on these pages— from a family's one-room cabin in the Catskills to a magical garden shared by neighbors in Oakland, California—inspire you to start making better, greener decisions for your own domain. All without sacrificing beauty.

1

The 100-Mile Parlor-Floor Flat

Remodelista editor in chief Julie Carlson shares how (and why) she and her husband, Remodelista CEO Josh Groves, furnished their apartment with designs sourced within a 100-mile (161-kilometer) radius of their neighborhood.

← Our flat has its original moldings, oversize windows, and cast-iron radiators, which drew us to the space. We painted the interiors entirely with Benjamin Moore's zero-VOC Eco Spec in Atrium White, and finished the floors with Bona's waterborne sanding sealer. The mid-century modern Thonet chairs are vintage.

↑ I feel more connected to my possessions if I buy directly from makers and learn their story. The hand-thrown planter perched on a stoop-sale stool is by *New York* magazine editor and Renaissance man David Haskell, picked up at a pottery show. The landscape paintings flanking the fireplace are by artist Rob DuToit, a longtime family friend on Cape Cod, where I grew up.

When my husband, Josh, and I moved to Brooklyn Heights a few years ago, we were in search of an apartment to make our own—we didn't want to rip up someone else's perfectly functional remodel or buy into an impersonal apartment tower. After more than a year of searching, we were lucky to find a brownstone parlor-floor flat that hadn't been updated in thirty years. Determined to source locally as much as possible, we modeled our renovation after the Slow Food movement and the "100-mile rule," which challenges us to eat only foods produced within 100 miles (161 kilometers) of home.

Working with our friend Malachi Connolly, a New York/Cape Cod–based architect and longtime board member of the Cape Cod Modern House Trust, we were able to sleuth almost all the new functional elements from New York craftspeople: a shelving unit from Atlas Industries of Newburgh; kitchen cabinetry from Pickett Furniture in Red Hook, Brooklyn; a steel lamp from Rhinebeck furniture maker Sawkille Co. We scoured the city for vintage pieces to fill in the blanks, and visited salvage yards for fittings.

Did we succeed in our hyperlocal-sourcing goal? In many ways, yes, but not entirely. We kept the tub and commode in the main bathroom but replaced the plumbing fixtures with new ones sourced from Dornbracht in Germany (on the plus side, it is a family-owned company, and its products are handmade). And by shipping some of our existing furniture from California to New York, we committed an ecological no-no. On the other hand, doing so meant we could continue using pieces we love—including the oversize dining table that served as our "office" when we launched Remodelista so many years ago.

The Cove sofa, from John Derian in the East Village, is based on a Sheraton-style antique and made by Cisco Home, an early-to-the-game eco-friendly upholstery company. Hanging over it is an oil painting by Rob DuToit. The 1960s Lotte Bostlund table lamp is from Cabin Modern in Brooklyn.

Support the Arts

The white oak and cold-rolled steel wall-mounted shelving system by Atlas Industries holds a collection of vintage pottery, oil paintings by Cape Cod artists, and blown glass pieces from various artisans we admire. Art and handmade elements work together to humanize a space.

↑ Scavenge, Scavenge, Scavenge

We scored our used Sub-Zero refrigerator on Craigslist; it still works perfectly and cost a fraction of what we would have paid for a new model. The vintage stool is from Etsy, and the sleek enameled steel trash can was a splurge: it's Frédéric Perigot's Frisbee bin, bought off the floor at ABC Carpet & Home in Manhattan and hauled back to Brooklyn on the subway.

→ Repeat Past Successes

We installed a wall-mounted Chicago Faucets tap with an articulated spout, a model we've used (and loved) before. It's well priced, American made, and incredibly durable. And for the minimally detailed cabinets, we turned to nearby Pickett Furniture (one of our earliest Remodelista advertisers, back in the late aughts).

Patch, Don't Discard

The fringed rug is from Prïvate0204, a Danish company that patches vintage hemp kilims, to charming effect. We sourced our six-drawer storage bed from ecologically minded Urbangreen Furniture in Brooklyn (now sadly shuttered); it's draped in an oversize Orkney linen coverlet filled with Sonoma wool from Rough Linen. The floor lamp is from lighting designer David Weeks, who manufactures all his products in his Brooklyn studio.

↑↑ Hold On to Heirlooms

The set of small silver bowls, which some might find old-fashioned, came from my husband's aunt. The Paul Resika work on paper of the Provincetown pier was a wedding present from the artist. The white bisque lamp is vintage, found in a local antiques store.

↑ Don't Be Afraid to Mix Eras

A classic Shaker-style peg rail hangs above a pair of refurbished Paul McCobb dressers from the Brooklyn shop Symmetry Modern, a good source for reconditioned pieces by the mid-century master.

Preserve What Works

The dressing room cabinets are original and retain their icebox-style door latches. The 1970s Marimekko dress belonged to my mother, who wore it to many a cocktail party on the Outer Cape. The vintage handblown opal glass Wohlert pendant light, sourced from LaNoBa Design in Jersey City, came out of a Danish courthouse.

↑ Find a Place for Everything

The pièce de résistance: a built-in niche for the kitty litter box (you may recognize our cat, JoJo, from the cover of *Remodelista: The Organized Home*).

← Beg, Borrow, and Steal

My friend and Remodelista cofounder Francesca Connolly donated the Jasper Morrison Glo-Ball Zero sconce and the overhead light, which had gone unused in a project of hers. We spec'd the most basic square ceramic tiles from US company Daltile, and set them in a classic running bond pattern (the same tiles appear in our kitchen). Out of view: the original toilet and Art Deco bathtub (a thorough cleaning returned them both to a sparkling state).

↑ Customize If You Can

For the office/guest room, Malachi designed a small built-in desk to fit discreetly in a corner; a local carpenter built it. We could have gone with a cheaper piece from a big-box company, but the slight extra cost for the size and quality was worth it.

↗ Maximize Small Spaces

Malachi, working with New York architect Joseph Vidich of Kin & Company, designed a crisp blackened steel railing and handrail, which were fabricated locally.

LESSONS LEARNED: COMMIT TO "SLOW DESIGN"

When we launched Remodelista in 2007, we were inspired by the Slow Food movement, which embraces the idea that food should be "good, clean, and fair" and soundly rejects fast-food culture. We asked ourselves, If these principles could be applied to what we eat, why not to how we decorate? Here are three ways to translate them for the home.

1. BUY LOCAL.
Source from community craftspeople and makers whenever possible. If you can't find products locally, purchase pieces from companies that have responsible manufacturing practices.

2. OPT FOR NATURAL, ORGANIC MATERIALS.
Wood, linen, hemp, wool—they all enhance domestic life and won't off-gas toxic fumes. (See page 224 for more information on how to choose eco-friendly textiles and other household basics.)

3. REJECT FAST FURNITURE AND EMBRACE TIMELESS STYLE.
The best way to avoid decorating regret is to stick to tried-and-true classics and choose well-made pieces that will stand the test of time. You won't be tempted to toss big-ticket items if you research your purchase to the ends of the earth and commit to a long-term relationship with your sofa.

The Hand-Built Homestead

In the Catskills compound of woodworker Brian Persico and fiber artist Hannah Haworth, nearly everything is handmade—including the house itself. Every beam of wood in the couple's home was carved from trees cleared from their land.

← Brian, here with daughter Celeste, used a mix of pine and maple boards milled from trees on the property to fabricate the kitchen cabinets in his nearby workshop. They're finished with linseed oil paint (a nontoxic alternative to traditional latex paint). The blue AGA stove was a Craigslist score. "We got it used and pretty beat-up, then did some fixing up to make it usable," says Brian.

↑ The house looks as if it's been there a long time, but the couple designed and built it themselves.

Like many young new homeowners these days, Brian Persico and Hannah Haworth dutifully documented the design and construction of their house on Instagram. But unlike most of their counterparts, they actually built it themselves—nail by nail, plank by plank. The Renaissance couple was uniquely qualified to take on the project: Brian is an accomplished woodworker and furniture designer; Hannah, a textile designer and expert knitter and sewer.

Their 16-acre (6.5-hectare) compound in Windham, New York, is still a work in progress. It currently includes their compact Colonial, a chicken coop, a sugar shack, and beekeeping hives, but the pair's to-do list remains robust. Among their future projects: a flower bed, a bigger vegetable garden, a garage, and an on-site workshop for Brian. "We really honor and pursue our curiosities, which is a bit risky but has brought us to the life we have and love," he says.

It may be a while before the two can finally cross off all the projects on their list. Between breaking ground and applying the final coat of paint to the house's exterior, five years passed, both their businesses grew (Hannah's online shop, handatextiles.com, sells woven goods, including baskets from Indigenous cultures), and their daughter, Celeste, was born (she's since been joined by baby brother Mario). But their take-it-slow approach doesn't deter them. As the saying goes, good things come to those who wait—and, Brian and Hannah would add, those who put in the work.

The first floor of the house is one open room that includes the kitchen and dining and living areas. Nearly every piece of furniture—including the dining chairs, high chair, and table—was designed and built by Brian. The refrigerator, like the stove, was a Craigslist find that he refurbished (note the wooden freezer handle).

⭡ Forest to Table

The ladles, slotted spoon, and tongs were all carved by Brian. The palm leaf basket is the work of a Mangyan weaver from one of the Indigenous groups living on the Philippine island of Mindoro. Hannah, whose parents were missionaries, spent much of her childhood in the Philippines. "The pakudos motif on the basket is believed to ward off evil spirits," she says.

↑ Counter Intelligence

Resting atop the soapstone counters are one of Brian's wooden cutting boards and several of his hand-whittled knives. The couple chose soapstone from nearby Vermont because they were already in possession of the sink, salvaged from an old-school science lab, and wanted the counters to match. In addition, "soapstone is something we could work and shape at home with the tools we have because it's softer than most stone options," Brian says.

← Custom Knife Storage

Brian is a knife aficionado: he crafts his own and collects vintage and antique versions. He made this knife drawer with slotted storage to ensure that they have a proper home.

Memory Keeper

The kitchen hutch holds tableware and a favorite wedding present: hand-painted ceramic mugs depicting scenes from their big day. They were made for the couple by Tyler Hays, founder of BDDW, where Hannah and Brian met while she was working at the downtown New York furniture gallery.

Hearth and Soul

The couple installed energy-efficient radiant floor heating on the main level and salvaged cast-iron radiators in the bedrooms. "They're backup for when we're away for a few days. Otherwise, the L. Lange woodstove heats the entire house the majority of the time," says Brian. As for air-conditioning, there is none. "In the summer, it's cool here in the mountains, so opening windows does the trick." Hannah reupholstered the sofa with handwoven textiles from the Philippines. The tripod lamp in the corner is from BDDW.

↑ Portal to the Past

Like everything else in the house, the pine door, studded with wrought-iron nails, is handmade. Brian, ever the purist, used a millennia-old linseed oil and pine tar recipe for the finish; it both adds a hint of color and preserves the wood.

→ Inspiration Everywhere

The hand-carved Douglas fir stair railing was inspired by the curl of family dog Kiki's tail.

The Orkney Chair
Brian and Hannah collaborated on the Orkney-style chair. He built the pine base, complete with a drawer and a pull made from a found antler. She wove the back from grasses and baling twine from a nearby farm. "Everything this chair is made of is from outside the house and our woods," says Hannah.

↑ A Four-Season Garden
No matter the time of year, Hannah and Brian wake up to colorful foliage, thanks to Josef Frank wallpaper from Stockholm's Svenskt Tenn.

← Bureau of Labor
Brian made this armoire out of bleached eastern white pine but used stained Osage orange wood for one drawer. The pine is treated with a pigment-infused natural oil. In his shop, he sells the piece under the name "Fin Armoire," because it's "as smooth as a dolphin."

Bedtime Story

Celeste's room is filled with tokens of love. Brian built the bed from Osage orange wood, known for its bright yellow tint. Hannah knit the beaver and made the pillow and duvet, both of which are stuffed with kapok and milkweed fibers. Together, they crafted the mobile: "I found a pine sapling in our woods—I'd been waiting for the perfect one—with six branches growing together from the base," says Brian.

↑ Natural Selection

A freewheeling potted citronella geranium and a dried sea fan are all that is needed to decorate this corner of the bathroom.

→ Behind the Curve

When there's a resident carpenter, your home can have next-level detailing: the family bath has an arched, paneled wood door and a built-in nook over the tub. In lieu of using off-gassing paints, Hannah and Brian applied a lime plaster, colored with earth pigments, to all the walls—"The lime is treated with olive oil soap to waterproof it," says Brian.

↑ Baggage Check

Hannah's collection of vintage *pasiking*, basket backpacks made by the Indigenous peoples of the Cordilleras in northern Luzon, Philippines, and traditionally worn by men on hunting trips, is displayed in her attic studio. Hannah, who is still in touch with many of the friends she grew up with in the Philippines, started Handa Textiles to shine a light on the crafts of the Indigenous cultures there and give back to their communities.

→ Home Work

On one side of the attic studio is a guest bed; on the other, Hannah's office area, an orderly space where she designs textiles and manages her online business.

One surefire way to live more sustainably is to make and grow as much as you can at home. The more self-sufficient you are, the less you have to rely on third-party, waste-prone corporations. If you live in a place that allows it, here are four ways to live off the land.

1. RAISE CHICKENS.

The couple currently keeps seventeen chickens—Araucanas, some Sebright bantams, Silkies, speckled Sussexes, and a Maran—in a coop built by Brian. "In the winter, we get anywhere from zero to two eggs a day, and in the spring/summer, up to twelve, though the hens lay all over the property, so we don't always find them. We keep our friends and family stocked with the extras," says Brian.

2. MAKE YOUR OWN SYRUP.

Brian converted a former chicken coop into a sugar shack (shown opposite). The couple taps the maple trees on their property for sap in late winter or early spring, then brings the sap to the sugar shack, where they turn it into syrup in an aromatic boil. They are able to make about 5 gallons (19 liters) of syrup a year.

3. HARVEST HONEY.

Hannah inherited the beehives from a friend who was giving them away. "Hannah sells the honey occasionally, but beekeeping is really more just for fun—and because it's a good thing to do, given the sad decline of bees in recent years," says Brian. "Plus, the pollinators have been a huge boost to our little orchard and garden."

4. PLANT VEGETABLES.

For much of the year, the family relies on Stoneledge Farm, just down the mountain from them, for their fruit and vegetables. They supplement their CSA allotment with crops they grow themselves—mainly herbs, potatoes, and tomatoes—and plan to expand their garden.

← Norwegian Round Stack

Brian chopped much of the firewood from trees that were felled so the septic system could be installed. He stacked them in a circle, a traditional Norwegian method that many believe is the best way to store and dry firewood.

↑ A Multipurpose Outbuilding

The sugar shack, where the couple makes maple syrup, is also used as a gardening shed and, in the warmer months, as a sleep loft for "adventurous guests." It was painted with yellow pine tar, a natural preservative. The door was salvaged from a barn down the road.

Casa Cannabis:
The Hemp Farmhouse

Filmmaker turned farmer and eco-activist Steve Barron lives in a net-zero family compound built from the very hemp that he grows. His eye-opening quarters are a model for the crop's potential future as a construction staple.

← Known as Flat House, the new farmhouse is the work of Practice Architecture, an emerging UK firm led by Paloma Gormley that specializes in exploratory uses for natural materials and low-carbon construction. The exterior is covered in corrugated sheets of compressed hemp fiber and farm bio-waste resin of corncobs, oat hulls, and sugarcane by-product. The cladding was developed on the farm and is available for purchase.

↑ "The plan was to try to contribute something for our world, our planet," says Steve, shown here with his daughter and her family in the conservatory off the main quarters. The farm's 53 acres (21 hectares) are now a certified-organic operation.

"I turned sixty at the same time my daughter had a daughter. That made me think about how badly we've been looking after our planet and ourselves lately . . . and what I'm eventually going to leave behind." Steve Barron—director of Michael Jackson's "Billie Jean" video and the original *Teenage Mutant Ninja Turtles* movie, among other things—is addressing a TEDx audience in London, explaining how he made the leap from film to farming. Hemp farming, to be specific. Hearing Steve's concerns about plastic in the ocean, carbon in the air, and the depletion of topsoil led his friend Fawnda Denham to make a recommendation: "She said I should check out a plant—a cousin of marijuana that doesn't get you high."

To say that hemp once held great promise is an understatement. For centuries, it was the finest and strongest fiber around, used for making rope, paper, clothing, and lamp oil. Betsy Ross sewed her flag out of it. But a century and a half later, it all but disappeared. In 1937, the "billion-dollar crop," as hemp was billed that year by *Popular Mechanics*, was slapped with a tax and ultimately became illegal to grow throughout the Western world thanks to its biological association with marijuana: though both are *Cannabis sativa*, hemp, as Fawnda noted, is weed's benign relative. So while petroleum-based-product development flourished in the last century, growing hemp—a plant that absorbs carbon dioxide (more CO_2 per acre/hectare, in fact, than any forest or other commercial crop) and requires little in the way of pesticides to cultivate (see "Hemp: 4 Selling Points," page 52)—remained illegal in the UK until 1993 and in the US until 2018. "It was almost entirely forgotten," says Steve, "and it's still stigmatized."

Seeing the plant's promise and underexplored applications—including its use as a building material and moldable alternative to plastic (BMW already uses hemp in its door fabrication)—Steve approached his new venture the way he would research a film, with the goal of bringing hemp products into widespread use. He and Fawnda, now his business partner, bought a derelict farm in Cambridgeshire, England, and—after being checked out by the police—Steve got a license to become, as he jokingly puts it, "a hemp baron." At nearby Cambridge University, he presented his hemp pitch and soon had a team of materials specialists on board to help. That was 2016; today, Margent Farm, the carbon-neutral R&D compound created from the farm's own crop (and where Steve's daughter and her family live), is itself a model of hemp's many uses.

The carbon-neutral house rises on the footprint of an existing cattle yard (alongside a raised shed prototype, seen in the foreground). Powered by solar panels supplemented by wind energy and biofuel, the dwelling was designed "with the aim of prototyping prefabricated, sustainable, hemp-based construction to be applied to larger scales of house construction," explains Paloma.

Grow Your Own Home

Flat House's two-story kitchen and other living spaces are composed of prefabricated wood-framed panels filled with hempcrete, a highly insulating eco-friendly alternative to concrete made with a mix of hemp hurds or shives (the woody cores of the plant's stalk), lime, and water. The painted cabinets are from Howdens, a kitchen company that converts its own sawdust into the power that runs its factories.

← Inside Out

Unlike most new construction, in which the guts of the building are hidden from view, Flat House is cocooned in what it's made of. Hempcrete has been in use for centuries but was further developed in France in the mid-1980s; it's been popular there and in Belgium, and lately has many advocates in the US.

→ Natural Whitewash

The hempcrete and its framing are treated with diluted clay paint, a chemical-free finish that prevents the plant fibers from shedding and provides a clean-lined look. The main house is just over 1,000 square feet (100 square meters) and has three bedrooms (two of them off the kitchen) and one bathroom—with additional work areas and a bath in contiguous preserved old barns. "I didn't want a big house," says Steve, specifying that he wanted it to feel like it was "part of the culture" of the tiny house movement.

HEMP: 4 SELLING POINTS

Once relied upon as a cash crop, hemp is a plant with a promising future: it's a renewable material that boasts an astonishing range of uses. Among its advantages:

1. HEMP IS A CARBON SINK.
It's fast growing, doesn't require much (if any) pesticide, and can be planted on depleted fields as a way of renewing them: its long taproots absorb carbon and nitrogen and replenish the soil.

2. HEMP CAN BE MADE INTO NATURAL BUILDING MATERIALS.
These include hempcrete, which forms the walls at Flat House, and hemp-fiber insulation (such as the HempWool made by Hempitecture of Ketchum,

Idaho). Hempcrete and hemp-fiber insulation are both pest-resistant and help modulate humidity; hempcrete is also naturally fireproof.

3. HEMP STRUCTURES HAVE EXCELLENT ACOUSTICS.
The atmosphere is notably quieter in a hemp house.

4. HEMP PLANTS CONTAIN CBD.
This is why many farmers have joined the green rush. (Hemp grown for cannabidiol, or CBD, is a different variety than hemp grown for its fiber and grain.) Margent Farm sells its own line of CBD salves and oils under the label "Hemp Will Save the F***ing World."

↑ Sleep Aid
The textured walls in the bedrooms provide the sensation of being cloaked in a blanket.

→ Work in Progress
The second-story loft space was put to use as Fawnda's office—as Margent Farm's brand director, she develops hemp products, while also continuing her work as a film and fashion producer. (Steve, too, still directs and produces films and television shows.)

The conservatory is attached to a renovated grain storage barn. The wall contiguous with Flat House is finished with a hemp plaster being developed by Gloucestershire-based biomaterials company Adaptavate using Margent's hemp.

↑ Something Old, Something New

Flat House abuts an old stone barn that holds solar batteries and a biomass boiler, which uses wood chips to supply under-floor heat—to heat with hemp, Steve says, "would take more processing and expense, but one day . . . Our future needs help, and I've learned there's so much that can be done with this plant."

↗ Indoor-Outdoor Living

The conservatory connects the house to the fields.

LESSONS LEARNED: CONSIDER EMERGING ECO BUILDING MATERIALS

Climate nonprofit Architecture 2030 reports that buildings generate nearly 40 percent of annual global carbon dioxide emissions, a figure that includes the manufacturing of construction materials. Concrete, steel, and aluminum are the top three high-impact culprits. So it's no wonder that the search is on for environmentally responsible alternatives. Fortunately, hempcrete is one of several candidates; here are five others.

1. BAMBOO
A grass, though often mistaken for wood, bamboo grows in most climates at a fast rate, without requiring a lot of pesticides. Light yet strong, and able to sequester large amounts of carbon dioxide from the atmosphere, it's used to make utensils, furniture, flooring, kitchen cabinets (notably by Ask og Eng of Oslo, Norway), and, in tropical climates, towering structures.

2. CORK
Familiar as bottle stoppers, bulletin boards, and flooring, cork also works as a natural form of insulation and as a building material now being applied to exteriors and interiors. Soft to the touch and light but durable, cork is the bark of the cork oak tree, and can be stripped and regrown without doing harm to the tree.

3. MASS TIMBER
Laminates of soft wood are being used to create a cost-effective and carbon-negative alternative to traditional concrete and steel construction materials. To create mass timber components, lumber pieces are sandwiched into superstrong prefabricated panels, beams, and columns that can be quickly assembled on-site. Already popular in Europe—Norway has an eighteen-story mass timber structure—the material is emerging in the US. An important feature: Mass timber will char but is not highly flammable.

4. MUSHROOMS
Mycelium, the vegetative tissue of fungi, is moldable and light. When dried, it's durable, waterproof, and fire-resistant. It's being transformed into leatherlike fabric (see Mylo) as well as bricks, insulation, lampshades, and packing materials.

5. RAMMED EARTH
The number one item on *Smithsonian* magazine's fortieth anniversary list of future predictions: "Sophisticated buildings will be made of mud." A construction material that has been around for millennia, rammed earth—dirt mixed with water and other binding materials—is being put to use all over in a range of building types, from multiroom houses to hospitals and schools.

The Historic House Makeunder

Designer Deborah Ehrlich's approach to her old stone farmhouse is born from a desire to live an uncluttered life surrounded by things that are functional and meaningful.

←The original part of the house, built out of local stone, dates to 1722. Deborah bought the place after living in Provence because it reminded her of France.

↑As is the case with many old structures, the history of Deborah's house is etched in its architecture: Early on, a large clapboard wing was added to accommodate another generation of the family. Years later, when Deborah had a newly mobile toddler, the fence was a gift from neighbors who were renovating.

At the age when most of us were haunting shopping malls in search of the latest teen trend, Deborah Ehrlich was collecting old tools. Farm tools, in particular. Designed for pure utility yet elegant, these handmade objects resonated with her.

Many years later, this principle of pared-down, practical beauty informs Deborah's own designs—and the way she lives. After earning a degree in anthropology from Barnard, Deborah apprenticed with a master sculptor. She then moved to Europe, first to study design in Copenhagen, then to work on a large-scale installation in France. She's since settled in New York's Hudson Valley, where she makes sought-after crystal glassware and wooden furniture that is simple yet refined, delicate-looking but actually very durable. And the eighteenth-century farmhouse she shares with her teen daughter, Willa, is in many ways like the Early American pitchforks and saws she still collects: constructed by hand from organic materials—stone, wood, glass, and plaster—and built to last for generations.

After Deborah purchased the house in 1998, her initial interventions were guided by a desire to uncover its original structure, long ago obscured when the interior was chopped up into tiny rooms and covered in wall-to-wall carpeting. Since liberating the interior of the unnecessary, she's been careful to treat the place with a light touch, adding only what she needs to make it her own perfectly functioning tool.

The exterior of the historic outbuildings, including the Dutch barn, are limewashed, and the house is maintained with nonchemical cleaners, such as Danish floor soap, and often repaired using historic methods—all of which, Deborah stresses, is out of practicality rather than a desire to be a purist. It makes sense, she says, to treat natural materials with natural compounds that are better for the health of her family, too. "I can see the approaches that the farmers who built this place used, and they are very straightforward and smart: often the technology involves nothing more than gravity. I find that kind of pragmatism inspiring."

The expansive main room has a snug living area at one end. Deborah reupholstered the Victorian sofa herself and had the pillows made from the remnants. The plaster triptych on the wall is by her friend artist Julie Hedrick. The bench is one of several gifts from interior designer Eduardo Rodriguez and Herman Vega, creative director of *People en Español*, friends who were downsizing and appeared with a truck of furniture when she had just moved into the house.

The Table That Launched a Collection

Purchased at a local antiques store, the 12-foot (3.6-meter) table that Deborah hauled home atop her car roof is an integral part of her story. It was here that she designed her first collection of crystal glassware, now handblown in Sweden. Today, in between dinner parties, the table serves as a centerpiece for displaying her glassware as well as her more recent design in wood: chairs of hickory heart and ash.

À la Carte Kitchen

Like most of the house, Deborah's kitchen is furnished with a mix of the reclaimed and the handmade. The Viking wall oven, purchased from a baker, is paired with a Miele cooktop from a Culinary Institute of America graduate. Each needed a little work when they got to Deborah: the broken glass on the stovetop was replaced with customized aluminum, and the original gold pull on the oven was updated with a DIY wooden one, a tiny detail that makes a perceptible difference.

The Ultimate Housewarming Present
A friend who shares Deborah's appreciation for vintage forms brought her the
antique farmhouse sink. Completing the tableau are maple cutting boards designed
by Deborah, a vintage light from Denmark, and a wall-hung knob of French soap
that she swears by because it's so simple and long-lasting.

↑ Windowsill Galleries

Deborah uses her house's generous sills to display vignettes of beloved objects. Here, her own crystal votives are accompanied by a French jug from her days in Provence; bowls from the tearoom at New York City's Takashimaya, her first client; and a plaster pinch pot that Willa made with artist-designers Che-Wei Wang and Taylor Levy of CW&T.

← Local Score

The kitchen's worn Saarinen Tulip chair came from a friend's yard sale—and yes, it always serves as a seat for Deborah's onion bowl.

→ Economy of Line

Deborah's work is inspired by how Early American tools like this pitchfork use minimal materials and simplicity of design to achieve maximum structural integrity. As with her approach to her house, her designs, such as this desk and chair, are not about building things up but about reducing. And her background in sculpture is evident in all her pieces.

↑ Tall and Skinny

The sparsely furnished bedroom allows Deborah to wake up in a space that gives her a visual fresh start. "What I want to see in the morning is the sunlight," she says. The lithe frame of the antique canopy bed spoke to Deborah when she spotted it on Craigslist years ago. Like her own designs, it looks delicate but is surprisingly strong.

→ Light Play

Deborah prefers old mirrors to new ones; "When glass is mirrored on the back like this, it gives a more beautiful light," she explains. Though the pedestal sink looks original, it was sourced from a nearby barn sale.

→ → Move Over, IKEA

Deborah designed the child-size painted wood sleigh bed years ago for Willa, who still uses it for reading and napping. It can be taken apart and stored flat, until the next generation is ready for it.

Deborah's designs are extraordinarily sophisticated yet entirely at home in her "rough and raw" old rooms. She may agonize over the form of a crystal bowl but doesn't get entangled in the world of choices when it comes to her house's needs: she seeks commonsense solutions and is an advocate for making whatever you need. Here's her three-part credo.

1. DON'T BE AFRAID TO DDIY: DESIGN AND DO IT YOURSELF.

Deborah contends that everyone has it in them to create simple objects, such as a side table built with hardware store parts and marine-grade plywood. Her advice to budding designers is to keep initial projects simple and follow your intuition. If you're not handy with tools, she recommends getting a local carpenter or handyperson to craft your designs.

2. ASK A PRESERVATIONIST.

"In Europe, centuries-old houses are maintained in a way that's efficient but respectful of the materials they're made of," she says. In that vein, to repoint the exterior, she used a period recipe for mortar that came recommended by a restoration architect. "Local historical societies are often happy to share old house solutions."

3. EASY CAN BE ELEGANT.

Deborah knows she's not an attentive gardener—and that deer will devour most of her efforts. Her answer? Lavender. Not only does it remind her of her time in Provence, but it's also drought-tolerant, and deer steer clear of it (and most other fragrant plants).

The Heart of Bed-Stuy

When you live and work in the same neighborhood, your carbon footprint goes down while community ties go up. Kai Avent-deLeon's very happening world is centered around just a few blocks in the Bedford-Stuyvesant section of Brooklyn.

←Kai and her family occupy the garden and parlor levels of their building and rent out the top floor. The kitchen, dining room, and living spaces take up the parlor floor, where all the hallmarks of a classic brownstone interior—intricate cherry moldings, parquet floors, towering ceilings—are on elegant display. "This is the first house my grandmother ever bought. She stripped the paint on every floor herself and loved the woodwork," says Kai. "She took so much pride in this space, and I treat it the same way."

↑Kai is pictured here in her sitting room. While the architectural details are ornate, her style—both in fashion and interior design—skews minimalist.

Everything important to Kai Avent-deLeon is in Bed-Stuy. Her grandmother lives here, as does her mother. The father of her toddler son, Che, has an apartment nearby. Her clothing store and coffee shop, Sincerely, Tommy, is on the corner of Tompkins and Monroe. Raini Home, her indie furniture store, is just a four-minute stroll away on Hancock Street. And at the center of it all (if not geographically, then emotionally) is her own home, a classic Brooklyn brownstone that she shares with Che and her husband, Nate Thellen.

Kai's grandmother bought the building for $60,000 in 1984, well before gentrification sidled into the neighborhood, bringing hip restaurants and shops. Not that Kai has anything against hip establishments; after all, she is the owner of a couple chic small businesses herself. But she's aware that outside investments in her historically Black community can come at a cost to its residents. So she and two friends launched Building Black Bed-Stuy, a fundraising initiative for local Black-owned businesses.

What it comes down to for Kai is protecting and celebrating family—both her community of Black neighbors and her own kinfolk. Her sensitively rehabbed home is a testament to this pledge. Unlike many new buyers, who breeze in and tear down and build out in the name of modernization, she has chosen to honor the building's history. Its intricately carved wood moldings remain in pristine condition, framing every window and doorway; the parquet floors are as shiny (and creaky) as ever. The home is much as it was more than a century ago—and that's just how Kai likes it.

Kai had all the walls painted white as a modern counterpoint to the traditional moldings throughout the home. It also helps brighten the rooms, which, in brownstones like hers that have just two exposures, are notoriously light-challenged. The living room, sandwiched between the dining room and sitting room, has no windows but feels airy thanks to a white sofa and beige rug. The art on the wall? White papier-mâché works by Kai. A sculptural black vintage floor lamp provides contrast.

↖ Welcome Station

Guests usually ascend the stoop and enter from the parlor-floor door, but Kai prefers the more casual garden-floor entry, pictured here, where a thrifted bench serves as a seat, landing pad, and display shelf for art.

↑ DIY Daring

Kai knows her way around power tools and has a knack for transforming vintage furniture. Take the floating lacquered black credenza in the living room: In her former apartment, it was a modest walnut dresser with legs and a rectangular shape. Rather than throw it out when she moved into this grander home, she glammed it up and turned it into a wall-mounted piece with the help of a carpenter friend.

→ Organic Shapes

Kai gravitates toward bold, functional pieces. Here, in a corner of the dining room, is a playful anthropomorphic chair by artist Kelly Infield. Above it hangs ceramic art by Kai's friend Jaye Kim. "It's part of her series on veggies," says Kai, who's vegan.

Ornate Meets Clean-Lined
Kai allows only select pieces—mostly modern, always artful—into her brownstone. The vintage travertine table was purchased for a couple hundred dollars online. The acrylic painting is by Kai, a self-taught artist; she calls it *Falling Flowers*.

← A New(ish) Kitchen

The kitchen was serviceable when Kai first moved in, but it was not to her taste. Rather than gut it, she simply made it over with surgical cuts that left the footprint (and cabinets and appliances) untouched. Among the excisions: institutional square-tiled floors, now replaced with rectangular slate tiles softened with a sisal runner from Armadillo. And, in signature Kai fashion, an antique rustic table is paired with a chair of her own design, available at Raini Home. (Everything in the store ships efficiently by flat-pack.)

↗ Useful Souvenirs

A new floating shelf displays some mementos from a trip to Oaxaca. "I always like to buy from local artisans when I travel," Kai says. The tulips, her favorite flower, are from neighborhood florist Olivee Floral.

→ A Nonplastic Water Filter

A stainless-steel Berkey water purifier is a worthwhile upgrade from the plastic filtering pitchers most people default to. It conveniently holds 2.25 gallons (8.5 liters), which means less refilling.

↑ A Touch of Gold

Vintage details continue in the bedroom. Above Kai and Nate's bed is a Japanese screen Kai found on Chairish; the burl wood nightstands were also sourced from the site.

→ Beauty in Utility

A rustic wire laundry hamper and a horsehair fly whisk from a trip to Kenya elevate a corner of the bedroom.

Sizing Up

Instead of buying the myriad products that fill every baby registry, Kai opted for the less-is-more route when she was expecting Che. Case in point: the garden-floor playroom—which "Che has the run of," says Kai—has a kids' table-and-chairs set, a few baskets for toys, and some picture books on the mantel but is otherwise a refreshingly refined space that won't need to be redecorated as he grows up.

↑ Passed Down and Upcycled

Kai has quite a few pieces that were handed down through the matriarchal line. "The bathroom vanity was my grandmother's. When Che was a baby, I used it as a changing table, and now it holds the bathroom sink." The steel medicine cabinet formerly belonged to her mother.

↗ Home Spa

Kai selected neutral colors and natural materials for her Zen bathroom. The Swedish folk chair is another piece from her grandmother, an avid antiques collector.

For her kitchen and bathroom, Kai implemented smart, targeted upgrades—as opposed to gut jobs—which resulted in lower costs and less waste. Here are three tips for a minimally invasive renovation.

1. STICK WITH THE FOOTPRINT.
When you move kitchens and bathrooms around, plumbing often needs to be rerouted, which can be expensive. Instead, try to work within the rooms' original layouts.

2. EMBRACE THE IDIOSYNCRASIES.
When Kai moved in, the bathroom was über-eighties. Most homeowners would have ripped everything out and begun anew, but Kai chose to simply give the room a face-lift. She kept the bidet, left the dated tub in the same odd angled position, and stuck with the cream/beige palette. But in her hands, the room now looks chic and polished thanks to new tiles and hardware.

3. SPLURGE ON MATERIALS.
Another upside to the noninvasive strategy? The cost savings meant Kai was able to splurge on things she really cared about: soapstone counters in the kitchen, zellige tiles by Clé in the bathroom.

The Commune Experiment

Photographer Aya Brackett and film director Corey Creasey traded the American suburban ideal of individual homeownership for a multigenerational cohousing arrangement. In this courtyard compound owned by several households, they've found a village in which to raise their two young children.

← The couple's daughter, Miya, harvests green beans. One neighbor is particularly invested in the group's vegetable garden and tends to spend more time caring for it than the others, but about once a month, there's an all-hands-on-deck call to pitch in with gardening tasks.

↑ Niko, the couple's son, takes a stroll with his sitter on the sidewalk outside the courtyard. Even from the street, the shared garden looks like an urban oasis. Legend goes, the walnut tree behind Aya and Corey's house (center) was grown from a single nut smuggled from Italy to America by the family who first owned the property.

In 1983, Alice Erb, co-owner of the Berkeley institution Tail of the Yak, a tiny, eclectic gift shop, convinced three of her friends to go in on a double lot in Rockridge, Oakland. There were mature lemon, walnut, and fig trees in the yard; four stand-alone houses; and a common courtyard and garden so residents could easily gather to socialize, celebrate, or commiserate.

It was an experiment, and one that worked brilliantly. Over the years, other friends and friends of friends have come and gone—and come back— but the quartet's original vision for intentional living has endured. Today, Alice counts among her intergenerational, co-owning neighbors a community organizer, a Buddhist priest, a food writer and chef—and photographer Aya Brackett, film director Corey Creasey, and their two kids.

"It's like an oasis," says Aya, who worked for Alice at Tail of the Yak after graduating from college. When one of the cottages came on the market, she and Corey pounced. Later, after having their first child, they moved into the largest building, and recruited one of their best friends to buy the cottage. Now Aya and Corey's kids, Niko and Miya, are growing up "surrounded by aunties," says Aya. "The best thing about living here is that they have access to all these households. Miya often wanders from home to home, helping bake something in one kitchen, doing crafts in another."

Their neighbors have become a second family. "On the kids' birthdays, they'll have a party with their friends, but they're just as excited for the courtyard celebration with the neighbors," says Aya, who's been known to borrow not only the proverbial cup of sugar but also a car. "It's truly a gift to live here."

Aya and Corey's house (outfitted with rooftop solar panels) abuts the common courtyard. Residents and friends gather twice a month for potluck dinners. Architect Tom Dolan, one of the original four owners in the complex, was so enamored with the setup that he has devoted his career to designing buildings that prioritize community—often in the form of courtyard housing (see live-work.com).

Garden to Kitchen
When the kids are playing outside, Aya and Corey are able to keep an eye on them from their kitchen, thanks to windows above the sink that overlook the yard. One of the most popular projects ever featured on the Remodelista website, the remodeled space has cabinets made from sustainably harvested cherrywood and a stove backsplash composed of leftover Heath tiles.

↑ Green Party

Anyone can pick what they want when they want it from the multitude of crops grown in the vegetable garden, which include tomatoes, zucchini, cucumbers, raspberries, peppers, lettuce, asparagus, celery, beans, and lots of herbs. The beds are framed with fallen branches, trimmed to size.

← Job Perks

Aya may have worked for Alice Erb, but it was Corey who first discovered the compound. He was employed for a spell at Alice Waters's Chez Panisse, and through word of mouth, found a rental unit in the compound. (Waters is a friend of Erb's.)

→ Sweet Success

In addition to these 'Black Beauty' plums, there are lime, lemon, fig, apricot, walnut, nectarine, and kumquat trees on the property. Most recently, the group added a kishu mandarin tree.

The Bay Area is considered the birthplace of the American countercultural movement, so it's no surprise that the region has been hip to communal living for a while. Just across the street from the compound is a more formal cohousing arrangement, complete with organized daily meals, scheduled chores, and strict bylaws. A communal way of life may not suit everyone, but many of its ideas, and these four in particular, are worth considering, even if your closest neighbor is miles away.

1. SHARE LAND.

Just because your property has boundaries doesn't mean you can't welcome others in. For instance, maybe you have ample acreage but little interest in gardening. Your neighbor, on the other hand, has no outdoor space and is itching to grow his own vegetables. Why not invite him to start a bed—and you can both share in the harvest? Or consider adding a gate between yards so that children and pets can easily visit one another. Carving out more common spaces from private properties translates to more interaction and connection between neighbors.

2. SHARE STUFF.

Cohousing communities participate in the sharing economy. When members co-own a kitchen or a water heater or a patio, they're decreasing their carbon footprint. Individual homeowners can do the same. Instead of every household buying their own extension ladder and lawn mower, for example, several families can pool their resources to buy one of each, to be used by all.

3. SHARE CHORES.

If you live in your own house, you're likely not going to ask others to clean your bathroom, but you *can* ask people on your block to participate in a neighborhood cleanup or to help with curb strip weeding. When done with neighbors, these tasks become less onerous and more like social occasions.

4. SHARE FOOD.

One of the tenets of communal living is sharing meals. For most of us, it's not practical to do this daily, but a weekly or monthly potluck dinner with neighbors is a great idea. Life slows down when you can regularly break bread with others.

The Work Oasis and the Family Cabin

Architect-naturalists Bretaigne Walliser and Thom Dalmas of TBo believe that greenery ought to be an integral part of how we live, wherever we live. Ditto natural materials, both new (the wool insulation in their country cabin) and salvaged (the sink in their converted Williamsburg factory).

← When a test revealed high levels of lead and heavy metals in the soil near their office entry, the couple remediated the dirt with ground-up fish bones and fish meal (which render the heavy metals inert) and topsoil. Shown here: the courtyard koi pond. Plantings include Thom's late father's dahlia and Bretaigne's late father's lilac bush.

↑ Thom and Bretaigne run their own architecture firm, TBo (they were previously FABR Studio). In their repurposed office, it took a mental leap to envision sunny spaces: "The windows were blocked, and everything was covered in grease," says Bretaigne. They used salvaged brick and wood for the doorways and introduced floor-to-ceiling glazing.

Bretaigne Walliser and Thom Dalmas are hands-on architects who like to not only design and furnish their projects but tend to the plantings, too. They created a leafy work space for themselves and fellow New York architects in an old brick factory surrounded by a cityscape of cranes and metal shops in one of East Williamsburg's most untouched, industrial fringes. An Edenic courtyard garden—inserted in place of the existing industrial waste—marks your arrival into their domain. The floor-to-ceiling steel-framed windows that fill the interior with sunlight look as if they've always been there, but they, too, are a new addition.

The couple and their young daughter and son are confirmed urbanites—and country people. In 2019, after a long search, they purchased 15 acres (6 hectares) on a mountaintop on the western edge of the Catskills. For the first two years, the family camped on the property. More recently, they added a one-room cabin with a vegetable patch and orchard; they do all their cooking alfresco. Out back, there's a solar shower and a Nature's Head composting toilet that they give a rave review. The cabin has provided them with the opportunity to experiment with new, eco-friendly materials, such as sheep's wool insulation, and to study their own woods and meadows in Thoreauvian detail.

Both their city and rural bases are mash-ups of their naturalist, high-design, and cost-conscious sensibilities. And both have an exploratory, newly rooted feel—they're emerging places where ideas are flourishing.

The architects opened up the space by exposing the ceiling joists and inserting a long skylight. They also enlarged the openings in the brick piers for the windows. The bamboo shades and bentwood Pagholz chairs came from the Swap Shop, a leave-and-take-what-you-want institution at the Wellfleet, Massachusetts, transfer station.

↓ An Improvised Kitchen

The team cobbled together a cooking station using hand-me-down stainless-steel restaurant tables and a salvaged range. The walls are bare scratch coat: "The construction industry tends to rely on Sheetrock and gypsum to solve all sorts of problems," says Bretaigne. "Some construction-grade wall surfaces have a beauty of their own and use less resources."

→ Orphans and Strays

The vintage ceramic laundry basin was sourced from Brooklyn nonprofit salvage center Big Reuse. Bretaigne stitched its skirt from "a piece of muslin that was lying around." The marble backsplash is a leftover from one of the architects' kitchen projects, and the faucets are industrial taps with copper piping. The left half of the sink is used for dishwashing, and the right for watering plants.

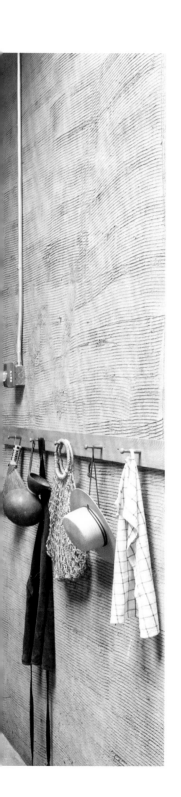

↑ Double Fire
The space is warmed by energy-efficient radiant heating under the poured concrete floors, as well as by a two-sided Rumford fireplace with a concrete hearth bench and rough stucco wall.

← DIY Catchall
The homemade Shaker-style rail was put together with a cedar plank and wooden pegs found online.

Hangout Room

A plywood-paneled alcove serves as the office retreat. The sofa is draped in a canvas drop cloth (easy to remove and wash). The wall-mounted ship's wheel belonged to Bretaigne's father, who was a Coast Guard captain based in Okinawa, Japan, during World War II.

A Catskills Kit Cabin

In the country, Bretaigne, Thom, and their kids, Isla and Theo, are outside more than they're in. They built their cabin from a post-and-beam kit: "These are ubiquitous as inexpensive garden sheds," says Bretaigne. "The kit we chose is from a small Vermont outfit and is made with hemlock, a local wood, with white pine board-and-batten siding. We drew up some modifications, and the company was able to cut a few things to size for us."

↑ Mini Mudroom

The storage chest by the entry doubles as a place to sit down and take off boots; wooden pegs and nails serve as hooks, and in lieu of a doorbell, there's a cowbell.

→ Upstairs Downstairs

The family sleeps in the loft and uses the main room as their living quarters. The advantage of working with a timber frame company was that the cabin's framing, pine siding, and galvanized corrugated metal roof could be flat packed and delivered by truck, but unlike with a prefab structure, Bretaigne and Thom had control over the design. They worked with a local builder to pour the footings and frame the structure, a process that took a few weeks.

Homemade Kitchen

Thom built the kitchen counter and adjoining bench of heart pine salvaged from turn-of-the-nineteenth-century building joists purchased nearby. The floor is tongue-and-groove white pine. A faucet and under-counter water canisters operated by a foot pump have since been added to the sink (the cabin is electrified but doesn't have running water).

↑ Keeping It Simple

The walls will eventually be insulated with hempcrete (see page 52) and finished with clay plaster, but for now provide built-in shelving. The stacking daybeds from IKEA are topped with Tensira kapok-filled bedrolls and pillows from Goodee and the Primary Essentials. The Achille Castiglioni Viscontea suspension light was on Bretaigne's design wish list; she found it at a Brooklyn yard sale.

→ Warming Hut

Thom sourced the Jøtul stove for free on Craigslist and extensively refurbished it, including inserting a new catalytic converter and sealing the door for efficiency. "There are cleaner ways to heat your house, but we use felled trees for firewood, and the space to heat is very small," says Thom. He and Bretaigne made the hearth from bricks being tossed from a Brooklyn factory, and found the fireplace tools at the local dump. A small GalaFire stove fan helps spread the warmth.

↑ Catskills Chalet

A vintage Swiss stabelle chair (from a Rhode Island antiques store) and Welsh milking stools (found on eBay) provided inspiration for Thom's scalloped banquette. The vintage trestle table and candelabra traveled home with the family from a trip to Wellfleet, Massachusetts.

→ Farm-Grown Insulation

The rafters are insulated with 100-percent pure sheep's wool from Havelock Wool, which the couple was in the process of cladding when this was photographed. "It arrived in soft, fluffy rolls of batting," says Bretaigne.

"Wool filters and improves air quality and absorbs and releases moisture easily while suppressing mold and mildew. It's also naturally flame retardant." (See page 298 for more on eco-friendly insulation.)

→ → In the Company of Trees

"The property encompasses a beautiful wafting meadow ringed by a mature red pine forest that gently slopes into a first-growth forest filled with beech, sugar maple, oak, wild cherry, and ash trees. Old stone walls trickle and weave through," says Bretaigne.

For every detail of their Catskills cabin, Thom and Bretaigne sought out building supplies that are safe, renewable, and locally available. "We think of ourselves a little like chefs working with food grown by farmers," says Thom. Along the way, they discovered three unexpected pluses to their approach.

1. THE WHOLE FAMILY CAN PITCH IN.
"A wonderful thing about using less industrialized materials is the friendliness of installation," says Thom. "We can do the work with our kids around—and with them as helpers—without needing to wear protective equipment, as you would with fiberglass insulation, for example."

2. THIS KIND OF ARCHITECTURE IS ABOUT TACTILITY AND SCENT.
"There's a sensuous quality to these materials," says Bretaigne. "The pine and hemlock are hearty and warm and emit a hint of sap; the wool gives the space a faint barn-like smell; and the clay wall finish will absorb and expel moisture, and have a smooth, cool, powdery feel."

3. NATURE NURTURES.
Carefully sited to take in the sweep of wildflowers and woods, the cabin looks entirely at home on its mountaintop, thanks to the fact that it's built from the area's own wood and stone.

The Net-Zero Urban Infill House

Set on a sliver of land considered unbuildable, this minimalist one-bedroom tower by Kate Fitzgerald's all-woman architecture firm, Whispering Smith, showcases affordable alternatives to status quo housing.

← The architects translated the familiar gabled suburban house form into a lean modernist sculpture. To avoid shipping steel-framed windows, Kate and a friend learned how to make their own with Low-E (low-emissivity) glazing. The standing-seam metal roof is insulated with SIPS (structural insulated panels).

↑ The material used throughout is "green concrete," which has high recycled content (for more on the subject, see page 116). Kate's partner, Matt Johnston, shown here (on the right) with a Whispering Smith friend and client, introduced native plantings and rescued the weeping mulberry tree from a construction site.

Kate Fitzgerald was exasperated—with how hard it is for women architects to make inroads in the profession, and with the way so much residential building (in general, and in Perth, Australia, where she lives, in particular) follows a bland and wasteful formula. Since graduating from the Melbourne School of Design in 2010, she's been doing her best to change these things.

Kate now runs her own "staunchly feminist" architecture firm, Whispering Smith, named after an old Western series "about an underdog sheriff trying to restore law and order." The group specializes in minimalist design using affordable, low-impact materials. And in leading by example: House A, Kate and her partner Matthew Johnston's own place, rises alongside a 1950s house on a sliver of leftover land, a building strategy known as "urban infill." The stripped-to-the-essentials structure was constructed using lower-carbon concrete, recycled brick, discontinued tile, and little else—the architectural equivalent of an inspired meal made from pantry staples.

The resulting 753-square-foot (70-square-meter) bungalow makes economic use of every inch, indoors and out: "We're capable of hosting a dinner party for thirty," says Kate. The bungalow also has some hard-to-see key features, including an underground garage; a rain tank under the deck that collects water for drinking and showering; solar panels; and an internal laundry line.

House A is part of a small Whispering Smith development in the Perth beach suburb of Scarborough that Kate, Matt (a landscaper with his own design/build company), and Kate's father own together. It's the first of three carbon-neutral residences on the property, and the first such dwelling in the area. The award-winning project is Kate's favorite to date: "It gave us a soapbox and megaphone." Take a look at what it has to say.

Finished in the same concrete as the exterior plus salvaged brick, the living area wraps around a courtyard. "Each space flows into the next; the only room that has a door is the loo," says Kate. "For 70 percent of the year, we live half outside."

GREENER CONCRETE

The most widely used construction material in the world, concrete is durable, versatile, fire-resistant—and responsible for about 8 percent of global carbon emissions. As the *New York Times* reported, "If concrete were a country, it would rank third in emissions behind China and the United States." Which is why there's a movement afoot to improve the mix that goes into concrete by using recycled ingredients. Fly ash, a by-product of coal-burning plants, and slag, a by-product of steel production, are being used as a binder

in place of expensive cement (65 percent slag content was applied here, giving the concrete its grayish hue). Of late, glass collected by municipal recycling programs has been added in the same way. And a company called Biomason uses carbon and calcium in its "biocement." Getting the building industry to change its ways is complicated, and a solution with widespread commercial applications has yet to be figured out. Search "green concrete" to read up on the latest developments and to find a source and builder near you.

← Furniture Included

A mezzanine bedroom gives the living room an airiness that belies its small footprint. To make the most of the space, all the furniture was custom designed as built-ins. Shown here are an upholstered steel banquette and tiled bench. The latter was made by Matt, a skilled builder; he and his team were responsible for the interior finishing. "Everything from the shell onward was Matt," notes Kate. "We'd be Whispering Nobody without his hard work."

↓ Shades of Pale

The kitchen and office extend off the living area: the window overlooks the courtyard bar. The counters and bench are white concrete, and there's an induction cooktop by Bora (the fridge and stove are in the tall cupboard with a sliding door). Kate notes that the white cabinets were recycled from the house next door: "We're millennials; we don't have money for cabinets."

This Way Up
A plantation pine open-riser stair—with an almost invisible steel enclosure—is set on a brick platform that serves as the music niche. The recycled brick is finished with Bauwerk Colour limewash paint. "We chose materials that are simple to construct and don't require cladding or extra finishes," says Kate. "The concrete will never need painting and will only get better as it ages."

↓ **Keep It**
The wall-m
minimal de
the gross p
require a c
are on the

The Hideaway
In contrast to the open main quarters, the loft bedroom is a secluded retreat. The soft palette, Kate says, originated from "a desire to have a space to unwind in that isn't saturated with trends or design features or glossy finishes." The house is cooled by a reliable daily sea breeze, cross-ventilation, and fans.

The Rescued Relic

The two aesthetes behind Toronto cult design gallery Mjölk unveil the hidden beauty of an abandoned stone farmhouse— and discover a simpler, Wi-Fi-free way to live.

← During the week, the family and their hounds, Atla and Aoife, lead an urban existence in Toronto; they escape two hours north to the farm on weekends and vacations. And during the COVID-19 pandemic, it became their full-time abode.

↑ The house was built from stones gathered when the surrounding fields were first cleared, and has a new roof of Canadian red cedar shake. A cornfield separates it from its nearest neighbors.

At Remodelista, we frequently cross paths with design purists, but few approach their rooms with the same down-to-the-final-detail commitment that John Baker and Juli Daoust do. The couple lives with their children, Elodie and Howell, upstairs from their Toronto shop, Mjölk, where they've assembled one of the world's most refined selections of Scandinavian and Japanese furnishings, past and present. Exquisitely crafted everyday items are their trade and passion. The two are self-taught curators and remodelers—when they met, Juli was a photographer and John a musician—and they often proceed by gut instinct.

That's how they came to purchase an 1840s stone farmhouse on 2 acres (0.8 hectare) near Prince Edward County that a parade of developers had run from. The fact that it had been left empty for ten years and lacked plumbing, heating, and electricity belied what John and Juli sensed: honest, pure design was lurking underneath it all. And at a price they could afford. "It felt like the last great deal in real estate," says John.

Once the house was theirs, they set out to celebrate rather than refashion it. The remodeling tack they took is one familiar to preservation-minded architects, who use the phrase "The greenest building is the one that is already built." That's because the environmental cost of new construction can be enormous. So can tampering with the layout: "Designers often meddle with the site plan thinking they have to present something original—and bigger," says John. "We kept the flow exactly as it was." Acting as their own contractors, they removed all of the intrusive elements—vinyl flooring, foam drop ceilings, particleboard walls— and brought the house back to what it was when it was built by Scottish settlers: no additions; not much in the way of modern conveniences, such as internet; only one bath. And then they made it their own with some of their favorite things.

The centerpiece of the parlor is a woodstove known as a *kakelugn*. John and Juli fell in love with these stoves in the historic stone houses on the Swedish island of Gotland. Importing all the parts would have been costly, so instead they had a masonry firebox and flue channel built and finished it with salvaged antique tiles from Lindholm Kakelugn. (For more on heating with woodstoves, see page 137.)

← Natural Glow

A hammered brass candle sconce from three-generation Swedish family workshop Appelgren shines a golden light.

↓ Age-Old Upholstery

The Arne Jacobsen Mayor sofa—designed in 1939 for a Swedish town hall wedding room—is upholstered in velvet from Greenguard Gold–certified company Kvadrat. Velvet is surprisingly durable. "It's one of those things that endures and looks better with wear," says John. The pine floors are original, newly sanded and lightened with Woca Wood Lye and white wood soap.

Set in Stone
Formerly a toolshed, the kitchen/dining room had a dirt floor, now replaced with concrete floors that have energy-efficient radiant heating underneath. Particleboard paneling was removed to reveal the original stone walls. The kitchen components—all freestanding and movable—were built by Studio Junction of Toronto. The "low-tech" wood-fired stove is an Esse.

↓ Mix and Match

The sink is composed of a reclaimed marble basin and a faucet of aged unfinished brass. The drying rack was neatly inserted into what had been a doorway. "We kept existing architectural features, such as this weird entry, and utilized them," says John. The matte Carrara marble countertops are shower surrounds salvaged from an old hotel (they came from Post + Beam Reclamation in Port Hope, Ontario). Japanese tools, including a straw egg carrier, and a trivet by Superfolk, hang on a Shaker-style peg rail.

→ Clear View

The kitchen drawers on the island and elsewhere have gaps that allow their tidy contents to be visible from several feet away—"so you never have to go searching for anything," says John. It's an idea the couple borrowed from Ilse Crawford, a design hero of theirs, and from woodshop cabinets.

↑ One for All

The house came with a single "washroom," and that's still all it has—newly glamorized. "The room is this size because that's how big it was," says John. "In lieu of a shower, there's a reclaimed two-hundred-year-old marble bathtub—it had been sitting out in a field." There's a Perrin & Rowe raw brass handheld shower in the tub: "We saved so much by not installing a separate shower," says John. The walls are painted in Pure & Original's Fresco lime paint in Skin Powder.

→ Wood, Brass, and Marble

Clockwise from top left: A white oak table by Studio Junction is fitted with a marble basin. The oak bath rack from London shop Labour and Wait is a modern version of a classic tub accessory. Toiletries are stored in an antique barber's cabinet. The high-tank, oak-seated toilet by Cheviot may look old-fashioned, but it's actually a low-flow model: in general, the older the toilet, the more water it uses.

↑↑ Loft Living

The attic was a warren of small bedrooms. Seeing that the partitions were literally just tacked up—"when people had more kids, they put up more walls," says John—the couple decided to revert to the original layout: a single room for everyone; their bed is just behind the rattan love seat. The space is big enough that back in the 1840s, the mattresses would be rolled up and dances held here.

↑ All in the Family

A sisal rug and rattan detailing unify the space. The kids' steel bed frames are from IKEA.

↗ Hot Air Rises

Heat from downstairs rises through grates to warm the attic—so much so that the family has discovered that their Wittus Shaker stove is usually unnecessary. "People always comment that stone walls must make it awfully cold in here, but we're not having that experience," says John.

A BETTER WAY TO BURN

From an environmental standpoint, wood-burning stoves are a big step up from fireplaces (which send a lot of hot air and sooty particulates out the chimney). Stoves are less efficient than, say, electric heat pumps, but the latest models are far cleaner burning than their predecessors; airtight designs with catalytic combustors, which decrease the formation of pollutants, work well. Pellet stoves (or pellet inserts for regular woodstoves), which burn compressed matter made from ground dried wood and other biomass waste, are a still better option. That said, heating with wood is not the greenest or healthiest way to go. For the latest intel from the Environmental Protection Agency (EPA), visit epa.gov/burnwise. And for more on energy-efficient heating, see page 299.

↖ Field Office

While the family was quarantining at the farm, John had an extra room on wheels built. It offers a place to work, a daybed, and, as with all of John and Juli's spaces, spots for display.

↑ Type Right

John comes to the office to write and paint.

← Art and Industry

Tools are stowed in a Shaker caddy.

→ The Rolling Getaway

The design is modeled after a British shepherd's hut (these days often used in the English countryside as guest quarters). John found nineteenth-century catalog images—and realized that nearby Amish carpenters had just the skills required to build what he was after. "Amish buggies and shepherd's huts both have curved roofs and steel wheels," he says. At an Amish sawmill, he was directed to a skilled woodworker who was delighted to undertake the project.

John and Juli approached their remodel as a collaboration between themselves and their abandoned farmhouse. The results may look dramatically different from what they started with, but the work the couple did was straightforward and, they insist, affordable. Here are their three essential tips.

1. PRESERVE WITHOUT BEING A PURIST.

When remodeling a historic house, the knee-jerk recommendation from most architects and designers is to rethink the layout: give the kitchen a more central location, link the rooms to the outdoors, and build bigger baths. It's a pricey, time-consuming proposition that John and Juli say can be avoided by creative tweaking—turning a shed into a kitchen, for example. That said, they don't preach devout conservation: what had been a doorway, for instance, can become a window or a niche for a sink.

2. USE PORTABLE STORAGE.

The couple entirely avoided built-in cabinets and even closets—they're expensive, and you can't take them with you when you move. Instead, in the kitchen and bathroom, they found a place for everything by installing antique glass-fronted cabinets that can easily be relocated. They keep their clothes in a large cupboard ventilated with doors of woven rattan, a renewable material.

3. PRIORITIZE CRAFT.

Juli and John prize useful objects made with care. By seeking out the handmade, they note, you end up with a collection of everyday tools and furnishings that are timeless and beautiful enough to put on display.

The Off-the-Grid Tree House

With help from friends and family, Grace Kapin and Brian Jacobs built a one-room retreat in the woods that rests ever so lightly on the landscape—and cost just $20,000.

← Grace, cofounder of maternity fashion line Storq (here with daughter Onde), is framed by one of three oversize pivot windows in the cabin. Much of the wood used for the project was cut from the eastern pine on the property, then milled and kiln-dried for construction.

↑ The structure sits on a hillside and is reachable only on foot. Load-bearing fasteners called Garnier Limbs, invented specifically for tree houses, are anchored to two pines to help support the cabin. These bolts are designed to allow the tree to grow and adapt to the added weight.

For a few years, Grace Kapin and Brian Jacobs were the ultimate weekend warriors. Come Friday, they would pack their car in Brooklyn and zip upstate to Sullivan County, not to bike or hike— but to build their very own cabin. Though theirs was an unlikely hobby given that she's in fashion and he's a product manager, they had a few key things going for them.

First, Brian's brother, Mike, is an architect—at Jacobs Chang Architecture—and the couple enlisted him to come up with a design that would be both affordable and suitable for amateur builders. His solution: a one-room 360-square-foot (33.4-square-meter) "half tree house" that is sympatico with the landscape, cantilevered on a slope using existing trees for support (thus eliminating the need for a concrete foundation)—essentially, a sophisticated tree house.

Second, the pair are by nature curious people, happy to spend their downtime researching building techniques and materials. They fondly remember watching YouTube videos to learn the traditional Swedish method of weatherproofing with black pine tar that they applied to the cabin's exterior.

Third, they were fortunate to have a rotating cast of "volunteers" who were willing to do some of the hard labor alongside them. ("We cycled through quite a few family members and friends," says Grace.) With their help, and using little more than shovels, hammers, and nails (and the occasional transport dolly, borrowed from a contractor friend), the pair constructed the cabin on weekends and vacations over the course of several years.

When Grace and Brian embarked on their modern-day barn raising, it was just the two of them. Today, they have two small children, Merce and Onde, who enjoy the bare-bones retreat as much as their parents do, which really isn't all that surprising. The babbling brook, the rope bridge, the endless supply of sticks and rocks—it all feels custom-ordered for the young and the adventurous.

Even from inside the shelter, the forest is ever present. With the windows open, cross breezes cool the cabin, an important feature, given that there's no AC. The hand-loomed organic cotton checkered rug is from Woodard & Greenstein; the OGK safari chair was designed in 1962 by Danish designer Ole Gjerløv-Knudsen.

Open Wide
The 8-by-8-foot (2.4-by-2.4-meter) double-paned glass pivot doors, which turned out to be the most expensive part of the project, were the only elements that had to be outsourced. Grace and Brian had a hard time finding a company that would fabricate them at that size but finally tracked one down in Red Hook, Brooklyn.

↑ The Corner Kitchen

The cabin is completely off the grid: it has no electricity and no indoor plumbing (the family uses an outhouse with a composting toilet). In lieu of kitchen appliances, they rely on a propane camping stove and a Yeti cooler.

← Coffee Service

A stainless-steel kettle from Snow Peak, the Japanese camping gear company, and a handmade mug by KH Wurtz (from RW Guild) elevate the morning pour-over ritual.

**A Chemical-Free
Mosquito Repellent**
On warm nights, the couple opens
the windows and uses a net to keep
mosquitos at bay. (The kids sleep on a
small mattress on the floor; when not in
use, it's rolled up and tucked away.) The
linen-cotton sheets and cotton blanket
are from Area. The bentwood child's
chair–cum-nightstand is vintage.

← Hygiene with a View
No sink? No problem. Father and son brush their teeth on the front porch.

↑ Building Connections
Several of Grace and Brian's friends also have cabins on the property, but visiting them used to entail hopping on rocks to cross the stream. The solution: a homemade rope bridge. "We strung up steel cable wrapped around big pines on opposite banks," says Grace. "Next, we fastened the foot planks one by one. Finally, we strung the rope between the handrails and the bottom cables, and added a ramp to one side."

↑ Forest Bathing

As their rescue Catahoula, Clyde, looks on, the family unwinds in a wood-burning Swedish hot tub (details opposite), which siphons water from the stream.

→ Going with the Flow

With no running water in the cabin, Grace fills an enamel basin with water from the brook whenever she needs to wash up or clean dishes.

One way to build a structure without negatively impacting the environment is to utilize techniques from bygone eras. As part of their design, Grace and Brian employed time-tested Scandinavian building methods to construct their cabin. Here are three ideas they imported with great success.

1. WEATHERPROOF WOOD WITH PINE TAR.

Instead of applying coats of conventional exterior paint, which is loaded with VOCs, fungicides, mildewcides, and UV blockers, they took a page from the Viking playbook and sealed the cladding with pine tar. The process wasn't easy—"It probably took us four weekends to complete, with three coats per board to achieve a nice, dark black," says Grace—but it was worth the effort. "We were worried that it wouldn't translate to the climate here in the Northeast, but it's worked remarkably well."

2. SOURCE AN EFFICIENT WOODSTOVE.

When it came time to choose their cabin's sole source of heat, they turned to Jøtul, the Norwegian stove and fireplace insert company with more than a century and a half of expertise in helping homeowners stay warm and create hygge. "It's incredibly efficient and effective and a pleasure to use," says Grace. (See page 137 for how to build a better burn.)

3. CONSTRUCT A WOOD HOT TUB.

The couple knew they wanted a hot tub, but not the bulky plastic kind that dominates the American backyard landscape. Their solution: looking again to Scandi traditions, they built a wood-fired western red cedar hot tub using a kit from Seattle-based Snorkel Hot Tubs.

The Bohemian Compound

More than twenty years ago, Yolande Batteau Hirche stumbled upon her dream living arrangement: an enclave built from salvaged materials by an artist, for artists. In her characterful apartment, with fellow creatives as neighbors, she's found a respite from what she describes as "the commercial nature of New York City."

← Yolande (right); her wife, Katja; and one of their dogs, Misaki, in front of their ivy-covered building.

↑ The pair of welded COR-TEN steel coffee tables ("They reminded me of Richard Serra's work," says Yolande) was purchased new, but almost everything else is secondhand. "The stove was architectural salvage and was integrated into the existing brick chimney. It heats all three floors," Yolande says. Also pre-owned: the 1950s black leather armchairs by Jacques Quinet.

The street on which Yolande and Katja Batteau Hirche and Yolande's daughter, Leilani, live is unremarkable. Cars are parked on both sides. Unassuming commercial buildings, now converted into apartments, line the road. Greenery comes in the form of curbside trees, but they are spaced so far apart that shade is at a premium.

Yolande and Katja's building, though, stands out. Two sprightly elms grow in front of the three-story former shoe factory, its brick exterior fully taken over by ivy. Standing at the street-level door, one can practically feel the temperature cool and a breeze pick up, as if the sudden and abundant foliage has created a microclimate.

This otherworldly scene is matched by an equally magical interior, thanks to the discriminating eye of Yolande, the founder of Callidus Guild, a luxury wall coverings studio that spins marble dust plaster, precious metals, pigments, and other earth-sourced ingredients into wallpaper and hand-painted surfaces. A fine artist as well, she's appointed the space with objects, art, and vintage furniture, much of which was acquired by trading her own work in exchange.

She and Katja, who were married in 2022, rent their triplex from Tom Clancy, a minimalist sculptor who bought the century-old building and the one adjacent to it in the 1980s and, using mostly reclaimed materials, transformed them into four units with the intention of creating an artists' enclave. That original plan persists to this day: in addition to Yolande and her family, the compound is occupied by a painter, two sculptors, a photographer, an interior designer, and a fashion designer; they and their various dogs enjoy impromptu meet-ups in the leafy courtyard garden. "Living here has fostered a sense of community and interconnected well-being," says Yolande. "It's a safe harbor for birds, insects, and other animals and always reminds us that happiness shared is happiness doubled."

Off the front landing, a single rough-hewn stone step, found nearby and lugged here for reuse, hints at the wabi-sabi aesthetic that awaits. The rope tassel is a nod to *shimenawa*, a Shinto symbol used to mark a sacred site. The hanging sculpture of slate, sea stone, pearl, and bronze is by Yolande.

↑ All That Shimmers

Leilani is perched on a Rietveld chair in the sitting area on the second floor. The gold diptych by Yolande is titled *A Love Letter to Agnes Martin*. "It is hand-incised, cracked, and water-gilded 24 karat gold over gesso, oil glazed, and framed in steel," she explains.

← Color Story

Yolande mixes her own paints using natural pigments. Here, cobalt violet, terre verte, and fluorescent orange pigments rest on a windowsill.

Air Ball

A vintage glass globe pendant light by Italian architect Carlo Scarpa is a rare spot of color in the otherwise neutral-toned home. (The light is from Bernd Goeckler, the East Village antiques gallery Katja owns.) While the wallpapers Yolande designs are known for their sophisticated, painterly surfaces, her own walls are beautifully basic—this is a rental, after all. Here, on the ground floor, exposed brick and stone have been simply whitewashed.

↑ Salvaged Slate
The black countertops in the kitchen are old chalkboards reclaimed from a nearby school. To the left, behind the curtain, is a quintessential New York apartment feature: the bathtub in the kitchen.

← Friends with Benefits
Every floor features work by the couple's artist circle. On display in the kitchen are ceramic pieces by Katy Krantz.

→ The Deconstructed Kitchen
Rather than install built-in cabinets, Yolande uses Japanese *tansu* storage chests for kitchen essentials. The large antique tansu holds serving pieces, pantry staples, and other necessities. To its left, on the counter, a small kiri wood tansu from the Meiji era houses a collection of spices. The dining table, in violet-stained maple with bronze legs, is by Yolande's friend Tyler Hays of BDDW; the vintage Danish chairs with classic paper cord seats are a Børge Mogensen design from FDB Møbler.

↓ An Urban Oasis

Gardener Benito Salazar has been tending to the plantings from the beginning, almost forty years ago, and even helped owner Tom Clancy excavate and build the courtyard garden. Like the interiors, much of it was put together using reclaimed materials. The stone walls were assembled from old cobblestone pavers salvaged from Lower Manhattan, and the terracing was created with soil dug up during the excavation.

→ Purple Haze

The shared outdoor space is multitiered and encompasses this roof patio and a mid-level deck as well as the shady ground-level courtyard. Yolande's family has easy access to the roof garden via a third-floor door, around which a curtain of wisteria blooms every May. "Living in this creative community restores us, and puts nature at the center of our lives," says Yolande.

Climbing Walls
The wisteria that winds its way around the property can all be traced
back to this mother plant to the right of the garden entrance to Yolande's
home (the door opens into the living and dining area). Benito planted it
here decades ago.

Urban landscapes have gotten a bad rap because of their pollution levels and dearth of green spaces, but it's a fallacy to think that city living isn't compatible with environmentalism. In fact, in many ways, living in an apartment may actually be more sustainable than living in the country. Here are three reasons why.

1. SHARING IS CARING (FOR THE PLANET).

Yolande and other tenants have a communal laundry room, bike storage area, and tool wall. They also share their outdoor spaces. This pooling of resources leads to a lighter environmental footprint.

2. CITY APARTMENTS HAVE MORE ECO CRED THAN MOST HOUSES.

Urban dwellers love to gripe about the size of their flats and lack of land, but when it comes to energy conservation and resource consumption, smaller is better. When your living space is limited, so is the amount of stuff you need to buy for it.

3. CITIES HAVE A HIGH WALKABILITY SCORE.

In densely populated areas, you're more likely to be able to get around on foot or by bike, bus, or train, all of which carry a smaller carbon footprint than driving a gas-powered car. Reliance on car transportation goes up for those who live far from a metropolis.

Tool Library

Benito's gardening tools are neatly stored on a peg rack in the ground-floor hall shared by the residents.

Upcycled Crates

The tenants have all contributed to this thriving raised-bed garden, filled with edibles and flowers. Milk crates are repurposed as planters. Nearby, upside-down exhaust turbines have been turned into hanging pots.

The Back-to-the-Land Kitchen Garden

A few years ago, photographers and food bloggers Susann Probst and Yannic Schon moved from Berlin to a village in northeast Germany. There, they transformed a rammed-earth settler's house into their own rustic-minimalist quarters and cultivated a biodiverse kitchen garden from seed. They're now close to achieving complete self-sufficiency.

←To impose some order in their garden, Susann and Yannic plant their crops in raised beds constructed from larch. They keep track of the plants (when to germinate the seeds, when to plant them outdoors, which require fertilizer, etc.) in a spreadsheet that can be found on their blog, *Krautkopf*.

↑In addition to growing a hundred-plus varieties of vegetables, the couple cultivates about seventy varieties of perennial flowers. Behind Susann is a greenhouse they built from a kit from European retail chain Bauhaus.

One way to jump-start an environmentally conscious life? Move to a farmhouse and live off the land. It's what Susann Probst and Yannic Schon, pioneers of moody, naturalistic food photography, did when they relocated from an apartment in Berlin to a "settler's house" in a hamlet (population: fewer than 100) in northeast Germany.

The couple describes settlers' houses as humble postwar abodes that came with large plots of land. "They were built mainly after World War I, but also World War II, and were sometimes made available to unemployed people or refugees to encourage self-sufficiency. The houses were often constructed from recycled building materials, due to a lack of goods at the time," explains Susann. The beams and fieldstones used for their own home, for instance, came from an old sheep barn.

In the same spirit of self-sufficiency, the two vegetarians have learned to grow their own crops from seed. They've discovered, through trial and error, how best to coax bountiful crops from their land, to garden organically without pesticides and herbicides, and to breathe easier. "Our life has changed a lot," says Yannic. "We are more conscious of the resources we consume since we grow almost all of our own vegetables. Not a day goes by that we are not outside."

The couple's new pastoral life has enriched their work as well. "In addition to being photographers, we're now gardeners and craftspeople," says Susann, who, along with Yannic, documents their home projects on their award-winning blog, *Krautkopf* (translation: "cabbage head"). And between homesteading chores, they even produced *Erde, Salz & Glut* (*Earth, Salt & Embers*), a beautiful book of seasonal recipes inspired by their harvests. "Here in the countryside," says Susann, "we have gained time and space that we would never have found in the city."

The raised beds provide a structural grid, but inside each, a degree of wildness is encouraged. Every bed holds a mix of herbs, vegetables, and flowers, for reasons both aesthetic (varying colors and heights) and agricultural (companion planting to discourage pests, prevent disease, improve soil, or provide shade). Partnering plants that can benefit each other is a great alternative to using pesticides and herbicides.

An Earthen Home

Susann and Yannic's settler's house was built in 1948, mostly from rammed clay, "so the walls are made of the soil on which they stand," Susann says. "What was created out of necessity at the time has a surprising number of advantages, such as temperature control and noise protection, strength, and durability. This way of building is not only environmentally friendly but also creates a healthy living environment."

↑↑ Meal Kit

Fennel, snap peas, broccoli, kohlrabi, and palm kale fill this harvest basket. To ensure a rich yield, Susann and Yannic mix their own compost into the soil at the beginning of the growing season, then fertilize with a DIY liquid manure (made from steeping stinging nettles in cold water) before mulching with a thick layer of fresh grass clippings. "The clippings provide protection against erosion and weeds as well as valuable nutrients for the plants," says Susann. They also help lock in moisture; as a result, the garden needs watering just once or twice a week.

↑ Digging In

"Gardening has had a significant impact on the way we cook," says Yannic. "We find the inspiration for new recipes and flavor combinations not only in our garden but also in the shrubs, hedges, meadows, and forests around us. We have never cooked so experimentally as we do now." While he and Susann grow enough to sustain themselves for a good portion of the year, preserving what they can't eat right away, they still need to supplement with store-bought goods during the colder months. Their goal is to achieve yearlong self-sufficiency.

↑ Patina Reigns

"Everything in our house is about textures, surfaces, and structures," says Susann. She and Yannic chose limewash paints by Bauwerk Colour in order to achieve an uneven, imperfect finish on the original brick walls.

← The Country Life

Since moving to the village, "there is no boredom anymore," say Susann, pictured here with Yannic. "We can let off steam creatively in all sorts of ways."

↗ Wait and Seed

The couple grows all their plants from seed, starting them in the greenhouse. "To see the first leaves sprout, to put the young plants in the ground, to care for them, to watch them grow, to harvest them—to experience this whole process ourselves is incredibly enriching," says Yannic. He and Susann collect some seeds, but most come from nearby organic nursery Gutes aus Gretes Garten ("Good Things from Grete's Garden"), which specializes in heirloom seeds.

LESSONS LEARNED: LET IT GET MESSY

Susann and Yannic try to prioritize the health of the entire ecosystem instead of just the harvest yield. The goal is to set up their land for success, then let nature do as it will. If you work with nature instead of against it, they say, you'll be rewarded with a thriving garden, not to mention less work. Here are three ways to do it.

1. DON'T CLEAN UP IN THE FALL.
Leave the leaves. Let grasses get overgrown. Don't cut back your dry and withered plants. They may look dead to you, but to birds, insects, and other small critters, they can offer food and shelter. Susann and Yannic delay cleanup until spring so that overwintering creatures have ample places to eat and rest.

2. FIND BUILDING MATERIALS IN YOUR YARD.
Instead of throwing out stumps and fallen branches, the couple works them into their garden design as seating and borders. Bonus: These natural elements can also provide habitats for small animals that are important to the health of the ecosystem. "We shelter hedgehogs and common toads, which eat small snails and their eggs. Tits are also very useful because they feed their young with fruit tree pests, among other things. Earwigs, lacewings, and ladybugs consume lots of aphids. Earthworms, isopods, bacteria, and fungi species ensure healthy soil," Susann explains.

3. GO FOR VARIETY OVER UNIFORMITY.
While a yard full of hydrangeas may look pretty, it's better for your landscape to grow many types of plants, because they will attract more wildlife. "By promoting biodiversity, you gain lots of hardworking garden helpers. In addition to eating pests, beneficial insects pollinate our plants, break down garden waste, aerate soil, and provide nutrients," says Susann.

ROOM BY ROOM

Lessons for a Greener Way of Living

Join us for a close-up look at five key areas of the house—the kitchen, laundry, bedroom, bath, and garden—and find out how to make them more planet-friendly. For each, we present crucial details to consider, ideas for easy improvements, wisdom from specialists, and accessories we swear by. Let's get started.

2

The Low-Impact Kitchen

When remodeling the hardest-working room in the house, prioritize green materials and energy-efficient parts. And if you're in maintenance mode, consider impactful tweaks, from swapping out plastics to clearing indoor pollution. For inspiration, here's the kitchen that architects Ruth Mandl and Bobby Johnston of CO Adaptive designed for their Brooklyn passive house (see the couple's green architecture tips on page 304).

1. Consider replacing just the cabinet doors. The IKEA cabinets here are fronted with painted oak drawers and doors by Reform, a kitchen company working toward 100 percent sustainable materials and practices. If you do decide to start fresh, cabinets of reclaimed wood or locally grown wood that has been certified by the Forest Stewardship Council (FSC) are the gold standard. Bamboo, a fast-growing grass, is also good.

2. Skip the granite. Three better choices: paper composite (the pressed-pulp surface often used in science labs; manufacturers include Richlite and PaperStone), reclaimed wood, and ceramic or porcelain tile. Responsibly mined local stone is also worth considering, as is Greenguard-certified Caesarstone, shown here, a product made of quartz.

3. Not all plywood is created equal. This pegboard wall is made of FSC-certified, maple-faced ApplePly, a high-grade plywood produced with soy instead of urea-formaldehyde or phenol-formaldehyde—the off-gassing of these common binders can have short- and long-term health consequences.

4. Potted herbs thrive in sunny kitchens. Instead of letting cut cilantro turn to slime in your fridge, grow your own; snip only what you need when you need it, and watch it grow back.

5. Any glass containers will do for pantry staples. Instead of recycling jars, save them (see page 282). For display and stackability, though, there's something to be said for uniformity: shown here are Fido jars by Bormioli Rocco.

Strategies to Steal

Swap in a Low-Flow Faucet

Choose one with a flow rate that doesn't exceed 2.2 gallons (8.3 liters) per minute, such as this one by Vola, a pull-out spray model for ease when cleaning the sink. To make an existing faucet much more efficient, simply screw on an aerator: they cost less than $20 and don't require a plumber to install.

Borrow from the Laundry Room

Drying racks come in handy in the kitchen for dish towels, rags, beeswax food wraps, and more. The standing version shown here is Skagerak's portable Dryp rack in solid oak.

Sobering Stat
The US is the global leader in biting off more than we can chew: discarded food is the single largest component taking up space in our landfills. Americans throw away nearly 40 million tons of food annually—that's approximately 220 pounds (100 kilograms) of waste per person per year.

Meet the Wool Dish-Drying Mat

Wool is an absorbent and naturally mold- and mildew-resistant material that makes a presentable gathering spot for drying pots, pans, delicate stemware, and other items that can't go in the dishwasher. This durable mat, from the Sonoma Wool Company, is made of undyed, 100 percent American wool.

Integrate the Compost Pail

Compost receptacles needn't hog counter space; here, a bucket with a cover stands in a tall drawer right under the counter. Its contents are dumped into a Subpod composter in the backyard for use in the family's small garden. On the fence about taking the trouble yourself? See page 181 for reasons to compost.

Appliance Lowdown

The average life expectancy of the latest stoves, dishwashers, and refrigerators is about fifteen years, so chances are good you'll find yourself needing to replace yours at some point. It's a glutted market—here's what you need to know to make informed, planet-friendly choices.

Stove: No Longer Cooking with Gas

Many US municipalities have banned the use of gas in new buildings. That's because natural gas, a fossil fuel, emits carbon dioxide into the atmosphere when burned, creating indoor carbon and methane pollution. (A Dutch study concluded that children in households with gas stoves have a 42 percent greater risk of developing asthma. If you have a gas range, always run the exhaust fan when it's on.) The recommended alternative: Switch to an electric range, or an electric oven with an induction cooktop (Ruth and Bobby combined a Miele electric oven with a Monogram by GE induction cooktop, opposite). Rest assured, you can now find high-functioning versions of both, and either will allow you to breathe easier.

Cooktop: The Case for Induction

These glass-topped, minimalist designs use electromagnetic energy to generate heat fast and efficiently: whereas only about 40 percent of gas burner heat and 74 percent of electric burner heat is transferred to cookware—the rest dissipates in the air—84 percent of induction heat goes where it ought to. Meanwhile, induction cooktops remain cool to the touch: they use electric currents to instantly heat the vessel itself through magnetic induction. Cookware with a magnetic layer on the bottom is required: cast-iron and most stainless-steel pans have this and work just fine (but glass, copper, ceramic, and aluminum pots don't). No open flame means there's also no playing with fire—for charring peppers, for instance. But for speed, safety, fine-tuned temperature control, and energy savings, induction wins the cooking prize.

Dishwasher: Efficiency First

Energy Star–rated dishwashers use dramatically less electricity and water than standard models. Surprisingly, machine-washing dishes is more energy efficient than hand-washing them—as long as you're using the appliance optimally (i.e., don't over-rinse dishes before loading, skip the machine's prewash dish-rinse setting, and run full loads).

Fridge: Consider Downsizing

After your home's heating and cooling systems, it's your fridge that uses the most energy. Pony up for a model that's Energy Star certified, and scrutinize the "Energy Guide" label, which lists the appliance's electricity use per year, as well as the US standard energy usage for comparison. Size also has an impact: Appliances scaled like SUVs are energy hogs. So unless you're feeding a crowd, go with a smaller fridge—and fill it with only what really needs to be kept chilled (some common things that don't: tomatoes; garlic, onions, and other root vegetables; stone fruit; coffee beans; and honey). Also know that empty fridges waste energy, while crowded shelves prevent air from circulating and lead to food waste. The happy medium: full shelves that still allow you to see what you've got.

Recycling 101

The best thing you can do for the planet is buy fewer disposable items. But given how hard they are to avoid, the least you can do is recycle the ones you do buy. Which recyclables are accepted varies from location to location; check your municipality's rules online and—this is important—actually follow them. Don't be a wishcycler: someone who throws it all in the blue bin and hopes it gets recycled. (For advice on disposing of hard-to-recycle items—think toothbrushes and mattresses—turn to page 326.) Then heed these four best practices to make sure you're recycling right.

1. Keep discarded cardboard and paper dry.
Water weakens the fibers, which is why recycling plants reject soggy cardboard and paper. If rain is expected, be sure to put a lid on your outside bin.

2. Don't collect your recycling in plastic bags.
Plastic film packaging, including not only garbage bags but grocery bags, dry cleaning sleeves, and newspaper wraps, can clog the processing equipment. This is why many towns require that recyclables be put directly in the bins (though some still accept recyclables in clear or blue plastic bags).

3. Rinse your empty food and beverage containers.
It's an annoying chore (as anyone who's had to scrape out residual peanut butter from a jar will tell you) but a necessary one, particularly if your town practices single-stream recycling (meaning you don't need to separate your recyclables by type). A half-full can of soda or a takeout container with leftover sauce can spill onto your paper or cardboard items and render them unrecyclable. Which is also the reason greasy pizza boxes aren't fit to be recycled.

4. Put plastic caps back on bottles.
In the past, we were told to remove and discard the caps from bottles before recycling them, but advances in recycling equipment have made that step unnecessary. In fact, it's now considered best to empty the bottle and put the top back on to ensure that the cap gets processed properly and doesn't escape. (Check with your municipality, though, as some towns have different rules.) Metal jar lids and the tops removed from cans get sorted magnetically, so they can be left loose.

Composting 101

Gardeners aren't the only ones who should compost—*everyone* should. Composting not only produces "black gold" for nurturing your plants but also helps reduce methane emissions, a significant contributor to global warming. How? Food and yard scraps stuck inside garbage bags and sent to the landfill don't get the oxygen they need to decompose. Instead, they break down anaerobically (meaning without oxygen), a process that produces methane, a greenhouse gas even more potent than carbon dioxide. So no more excuses—here are four ways anyone can compost.

1. Sign up for your local composting program. If your municipality offers compost pickup, all you need to do is collect your scraps in a covered receptacle. If your town or city doesn't have a compost program, lobby your city council to start one.

2. Seek out private compost-pickup services. Most of these businesses offer weekly or biweekly pickups of scraps, depending on your needs. They do the dirty work, and you get to reap the rewards in the form of free compost come spring, if you want it (if not, your share will be put to good use).

3. Donate to groups that need compost. You can drop off food scraps and other compostables at composting sites, farmers' markets, and community gardens. Chances are good there's one near you.

4. Compost at home. Get a tumbler, compost bin, or worm composter for your backyard and learn how to make your own black gold. (For a great tutorial on how to start, check out epa.gov/recycle/composting-home.) No outdoor space? Consider a countertop electric composter, which dehydrates and grinds up food waste, turning it into a methane-free soil amendment in hours.

---

11 SURPRISING COMPOSTABLES

The bulk of your compostables will likely be food scraps and gardening waste, but some items from beyond the kitchen and yard can also be tossed into your compost bin. Here are some examples you may not know about. (If you're sending your compostables to a third-party composter, be sure to check its list of acceptable waste. And note: Bigger items should be shredded or cut up for faster decomposition.)

1. Clothing and fabric made from 100 percent natural fibers
2. Coffee grounds and paper coffee filters
3. Corks from wine bottles
4. Cotton balls and swabs made from 100 percent cotton
5. Paper cupcake and muffin wrappers
6. Dryer lint (from natural materials only, not synthetics)
7. Human and pet hair
8. Latex balloons and gloves
9. Natural loofahs
10. Uncoated paper and cardboard products, including paper towels
11. Wooden toothpicks and bamboo skewers

Who is he? David Tanis is a cookbook author, chef (formerly of Chez Panisse), and *New York Times* columnist. But what has particularly endeared him to us is his amazing, tiny home kitchen in New York City's East Village. Charmingly low-tech and impressively economical, it's appointed with cast-off furniture (in lieu of built-in cabinets) and vintage kitchen tools. In his cooking, too, he applies the same waste-conscious, back-to-basics ethos.

Ask the Expert
David Tanis

How can we all adopt more sustainable kitchen habits?

1. Cook from the market. David spent some time living in Paris, where he fully leaned into the French concept of cooking what's freshest *au marché* (his most recent book is titled *Market Cooking*, in fact). When he returned stateside, he continued his Parisian habits, opting to have only a small under-the-counter fridge to encourage more frequent market visits and, ultimately, less food waste.

2. Shop the perimeter. When you do go to a giant grocery store, David advises, stick to "the outer edges, where the produce, dairy, butcher, and fish departments are apt to be. Aim for real food, always—better for health, better for the planet."

3. Bulk up. By all means, buy in bulk, but don't buy willy-nilly in excess. "I definitely get the large size of certain things," says David. "I like to have a 10-pound [4.5-kilogram] bag of basmati rice on hand, for instance, and an extra-big bag of onions. Same for pasta, large cans of salted Italian anchovies, and beans. I always have a lot of dried beans on hand; they're so much better than canned, and so easy to cook. And just as important: buying wine by the case."

4. Store perishables properly. "Cool, dark, and dry is the rule," says David, as heat, sunlight, and moisture can accelerate spoilage. Wrap bunched fresh herbs—rosemary, thyme, sage, cilantro, parsley—in a damp rag or paper towel before storing them in a lidded container in the fridge. "This prolongs freshness," he notes. As for bread: "Don't buy sliced bread, which is prone to go moldy; if you do, store it in the refrigerator or freezer. Whole loaves are better—wrap them in kitchen towels and keep them at room temperature."

5. Eat less meat. The livestock industry is responsible for 14.5 percent of greenhouse gases emitted worldwide, according to the UN. David says it's time to cut back on our intake of animal protein. "Broadly speaking, most cultures use far less meat than the amount commonly served in the US. A little meat is used for flavoring, and the other ingredients are predominantly vegetables, grains, or legumes. These are good habits to emulate."

6. Commit to leftovers. "Lots of food just sits in the fridge and languishes. Last night's dinner can be today's lunch salad. Broth can be made with scraps of meat and vegetables. Leftovers from a main course can become the next night's side dish."

7. Compost instead of trashing. "Even the most diligent cook can't possibly use up all the vegetable scraps and trimmings. I feel much better knowing it's going to the compost bin rather than the landfill." Storing a bin or bag of compost in the freezer is a good small kitchen trick that prevents flies and odors. (See page 181 for more on composting.)

8. Keep tools simple and manual. "I avoid using electric appliances, if at all possible. I have never had a microwave oven—it's easier to heat up food in a pan on the stove," says David. He has a particular fondness for the mortar and pestle: "I have a good dozen in my kitchen in many different sizes. Any number of kitchen chores can be achieved with the duo: pounding garlic and anchovies for a quick pasta sauce, smashing dried bread for a handful of bread crumbs, grinding spices." His favorite mortar? The Japanese *suribachi*: "They're a great all-purpose mortar made of lightweight ceramic, and the interior is scored to be abrasive, perfect for grinding sesame seeds."

9. End your reliance on nonstick pans. Nonstick pans need to be replaced every few years (the coating deteriorates and can leach toxins), more often if you cook with high heat. "Cast-iron pans are better," says David. "They last forever and can become heirlooms. For that matter, it's worth looking for vintage cast-iron pans, pots, and Dutch ovens." Another good option: carbon-steel cookware, which has many of the same attributes as cast iron but is lighter.

Kitchen Tool Kit
Our Favorite Low-Impact Accessories

1. Aplat organic cotton bowl covers, secured with drawstrings in place of elastic (which takes an estimated five hundred years to decompose); aplat.com.

2. Waxed linen food wraps, to be used in place of throwaway plastic wrap. Wax Atelier's are tinted with natural dyes made from flowers, roots, and bark; waxatelier.com.

3. Waxed canvas grocery tote by Waam, a mom-and-pop workshop in rural Minnesota; waamindustries.com.

4. Classic French net market bag by Filt—light enough to carry with you always; flotsamandfork.com.

5. Wool dish-drying mat, a streamlined option for drying dishes. Companion linen outer sleeve available; sonomawoolcompany.com.

6. Dishcloth of knit cotton for extra absorbency; solwangdesign.dk.

7. Ardent Goods bamboo pot brush and solid dish soap in reusable porcelain container; ardentgoods.co.

8. Wool dish sponges—naturally antimicrobial and compostable—from Echoview Fiber Mill, a LEED- and Living Wage–certified company in Weaverville, North Carolina; echoviewnc.com.

9. Reusable organic cotton UNpaper towels; marleysmonsters.com.

10. Produce bags of organic cotton by Dans le Sac and the Earthling Co.; danslesac.co and theearthlingco.com.

11. Linen and burlap sponges with cotton filling: use as you would familiar polyester sponges; ardentgoods.co.

12. Organic jersey cotton napkins from Alabama Chanin, a pioneering ethical fashion company in Florence, Alabama, that leaves no scraps to waste; alabamachanin.com.

13. Lovett Sundries dishwashing powder, made by the Pittsburgh apothecary with four ingredients: washing soda, borax, sea salt, and citric acid; lovettsundries.com.

14. Wood-handled natural-fiber scrub brushes; salter.house.

15. Iris Hantverk cleaning cloth composed of recycled waffle-weave cotton; salter.house.

16. Kitchen scissors by sixty-year-old Japanese scissor workshop Toribe Seisakusho—these come apart for cleaning and sharpening; jinenstore.com.

17. Cast-iron skillet by Smithey Ironware of Charleston, South Carolina: forged from recycled iron to last indefinitely; smithey.com.

18. Enamelware compost bin by Net Zero Co., with a 1.6-gallon (6-liter) capacity and an odor-absorbing charcoal filter in the lid; netzerocompany.com.

19. Indian tiffin, a multitiered, stainless-steel storage container; abroadmodern.com.

20. Fido glass jar by Bormioli Rocco—like the ones that line the shelves on page 174; bormiolirocco.com.

21. Waxed linen food bags by Wax Atelier; waxatelier.com.

22. Glass reusable straws, sized for smoothies; hummingbirdstraws.com.

Coffee and Tea Tool Kit

Our Favorite Low-Impact Accessories

1. **Biodegradable paper tea filters** for on-the-go single servings of loose-leaf tea; bellocqtea.com.

2. **Ceramic sugar bowl and brass spoon:** the bowl is by Copenhagen design studio Frama, and the spoon is from Fog Linen; framacph.com and shop-foglinen.com.

3. **Fog Linen pot holders** made from linen remnants; shop-foglinen.com.

4. **Stainless-steel snack containers** by Sidekick, repurposed to hold tea leaves; helenmilan.com.

5. **Glass teapot with strainer,** first designed in 1931 by Wilhelm Wagenfeld for Jenaer Glas in Germany; crystalclassics.com.

6. **Wood tea accessories:** a beechwood coffee/tea scoop from wildminimalist.com; a citrus reamer from heaveninearth.com; and a honey dipper from HandyHousewares on Etsy.

7. **Small-batch loose-leaf teas** from sustainability-minded farms. Pictured are teas from two small, eco-conscious tea companies: Leaves and Flowers in California and Daphnis and Chloe in Greece; leavesandflowers.com and daphnisandchloe.com.

8. **Bamboo-handled tea strainer,** handmade in Japan; canoe.design.

9. **Manual metal coffee grinder** by Timemore, plastic-free and durable; prima-coffee.com.

10. **Enamelware canisters with airtight ash wood lids from Riess,** made in a carbon-neutral facility in Austria; ameico.com.

11. **Stainless-steel coffee/tea scoop** with a handle that doubles as a bag clip; from HandyHousewares on Etsy.

12. **Bamboo matcha tea set;** from BambooMN on Etsy.

13. **Ceramic to-go cup** with silicone lid and sleeve from Campfire Pottery in Maine; campfirepottery.com.

14. **Rush trivet** handwoven in Japan; helenmilan.com.

15. **Bodum's Melior electric kettle,** with a stainless-steel body and a cork knob and handle; bodum.com.

16. **Chemex pour-over coffeemaker with glass handle;** chemexcoffeemaker.com.

17. **Reusable coffee filters by CoffeeSock,** made from cotton that is certified organic by the Global Organic Textiles Standard (GOTS). They last up to a year with daily use, and can be composted at the end of their life; coffeesock.com.

18. **Hasami creamer,** designed by Takuhiro Shinomoto of LA's Tortoise General Store and produced in a region of Japan known for its pottery; shop.tortoisegeneral store.com.

The Low-Impact Laundry Room

Small changes to your wash routine can make a big difference. With its focus on practical, simple approaches, this utility closet created by interior designer Glenn Ban for shopkeeper Carrie Schei's home in Sag Harbor, New York, offers inspiration for more environmentally sound laundering habits.

1. Old can be better than new. Carrie's vintage wicker laundry basket looks and feels better than a plastic bin. Plus, when you buy secondhand, you're potentially saving something that would otherwise get tossed. (See our "Vintage 75" starting on page 240 for more ideas on when and where to shop used.)

2. Go with a front-loader. According to Energy Star, a front-loading washing machine uses 50 percent less energy and 25 percent less water than a top loader. And be sure the machine bears the Energy Star logo. Certified washing machines use about 25 percent less energy than conventional models; certified dryers, 20 percent less.

3. Hang a cloth towel nearby to keep surfaces clean instead of reaching for paper towels.

4. Hand-wash what you can. Bypass dry cleaning, which relies on chemical solvents that have been found to be carcinogenic, and instead spot clean or hand-wash your woolens and delicates. A classic washboard is useful for stain removal.

5. There are benefits to skipping the dryer. Air-drying takes a bit more time and effort, but this oldfangled method helps garments last longer *and* trims your energy bill.

6. Pick up a needle and thread. Have a sewing kit at the ready—and commit to mending more and buying less. Or turn your worn-out clothing into something useful (like the striped rug here, available at Lostine, made from old suit fabric).

7. Seek out nonplastic cleaning tools. They're hardworking and compostable—better-looking, too. This oak caddy is from the Ro Collection. (For more suggestions, see page 196.)

Strategies to Steal

Compost Your Lint

Stop throwing out the dryer lint. For successful composting, there needs to be a mix of green (e.g., food waste) and brown (e.g., dry plant material); lint falls under the brown category and can help you achieve the right composition for decomposition. (Just make sure the batch of lint you're collecting is from natural fabrics only, as you wouldn't want to compost lint that may include microplastics from synthetic materials.) Keep a container on hand as a lint receptacle (this covered canister is from Salter House), and add the contents to your compost heap.

Opt for Clean Ingredients

When it comes to detergents, look for a short list of familiar ingredients—baking soda, washing soda, castile soap—and nonplastic packaging. As for laundry boosters, all you really need is borax (which deodorizes and whitens) and distilled white vinegar (which softens and whitens, and is good for cleaning the washing machine, too). When using the dryer, toss in a trio of wool dryer balls—they speed the process, separate and fluff, and prevent static. Add a few drops of essential oil to your dryer balls for a subtle fragrance.

Get the Hang of It

Aside from lowering your energy consumption, there's another reason to air-dry your laundry: fabrics degrade with each session in the dryer (think about how much lint is captured in each load). Air-drying is far less taxing on textiles and will help extend the life of your clothing. Turn the page for rack sources.

Stop the Shed

Each time you do a load of laundry, hundreds of thousands of microfibers, invisible to the naked eye, end up in our rivers and seas, where they are ingested by wildlife; they've even made their way into our drinking water. And because so much clothing is made of synthetic materials these days, microfibers are one of the main sources of plastics pollution in our waters. (That's a strong case for wearing natural fibers only.) Fortunately, there are ways to minimize shedding: Tossing a Cora Ball (shown here) into the wash captures about 25 percent of the microfibers in each load and also helps reduce shedding. And while we wait for washing machines to be redesigned, add a filter like the Filtrol to your washing machine discharge hose to stop more of these filaments from polluting our waterways.

Air-Drying, 3 Ways

Owning a dryer isn't at all common outside the US. One main reason: frugality. An inefficient electric clothes dryer can use as much energy annually as a refrigerator, washer, and dishwasher combined. We think it's time to universally bring back clotheslines and drying racks. Here are three favorite styles that work even in tight spaces.

1. Collapsible

Ideal for everything from dish towels to wet bathing suits, Iris Hantverk's simple birch drying rack has adjustable bars and folds flat.

2. Wall-Mounted

This Amish-made accordion design from Saving Shepherd of Pennsylvania has a small footprint and an impressive reach. Below it is a Mavis & Osborn hamper made of linen and recycled steel from Kept Home..

3. Suspended Overhead

From Australian company George & Willy, this version of a classic is hung from the ceiling. Here, Glenn's son, Charlie, shows how it can be lowered via a pulley for easy access and raised to allow laundry to dry where it's warmer (remember, hot air rises).

3

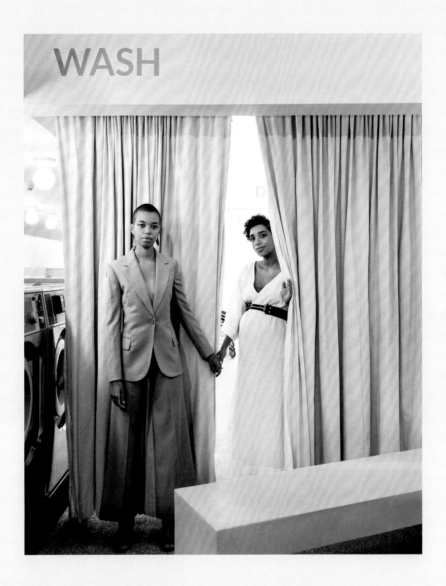

WASH

Who are they? Born and raised in Germany, Corinna and Theresa Williams are the sisters behind the eco-friendly Williamsburg, Brooklyn, laundromat Celsious. Frustrated with the dingy laundromats they encountered in the States, they left careers in graphic design and fashion, respectively, to open a well-designed and welcoming laundry-meets-lounge that champions sustainable best practices. At Celsious, customers get a complimentary cup of natural laundry powder with each load, and can head upstairs to the mezzanine for kombucha while they wait for their wash.

Ask the Experts
Corinna and Theresa Williams

What are best practices for a greener laundry routine?

1. Stop using fabric softeners and dryer sheets. "They're bad for the planet, bad for your health, and ultimately not necessary," says Theresa. Instead, add distilled white vinegar to your wash as a natural softener.

2. Choose nontoxic laundry soaps. "Conventional detergents usually contain a mix of endocrine disruptors, neurotoxins, and cancer-causing ingredients," notes Corinna. "The petroleum-derived synthetic scents of most conventional detergents are designed to stick to your clothes. Not only will you carry all these chemicals against your skin, but you will also breathe them in as they become airborne."

3. Wash less frequently. Most clothes don't need to be laundered after each wear. The less you wash, the less water and energy are consumed, *and* the less your clothing sheds microfibers.

4. Switch to cold water. Unless your laundry is seriously dirty, it will still come out clean with a cold wash. Heating water consumes 90 percent of the energy used during a wash cycle, so even setting your machine to "warm" instead of "hot" can make a notable difference.

5. Dry smart. First, make sure the spin cycle on your washer is set to "high" to ensure that as much moisture as possible gets extracted. "Then, if you're going to use the dryer, use the lowest temperature, if possible," advises Theresa. Running the machine for a longer time at a lower temperature is more efficient than running it faster at a higher temp.

6. Just say no to dry cleaning. "We've seen 'Dry Clean Only' tags on pretty much everything, from 100 percent cotton garments to cellulose-fiber-based textiles made of rayon or lyocell. And a lot of wool and cashmere sweaters," says Corinna. "All of the above can be washed with water and do not require the use of chemical solvents, which is what dry cleaning is." If you must patronize a dry cleaner, find one that either uses liquid carbon dioxide (a safe, naturally occurring gas) or employs the wet-cleaning method, which relies on nontoxic, biodegradable detergents.

Laundry Tool Kit

Our Favorite Low-Impact Accessories

1. **Wooden clothespins,** unfinished and ready to weather in the sun; from Le Box Boutique on Etsy.

2. **Retractable clothesline,** perfect for air-drying laundry indoors in small spaces; valsanusa.com.

3. **Cotton outdoor clothesline** by Librett Durables of New York, in the cording business since 1947; jamaligarden.com.

4. **The Laundress sweater comb,** with a cedarwood handle, to de-pill cashmere and other delicate knits; thelaundress.com.

5. **Purl Soho's sweater rake** for woolens, including sweaters, coats, and blankets; purlsoho.com.

6. **Purl Soho's sweater soap,** made from saponified organic plant-based oils, for hand- or machine-washing sweaters; purlsoho.com.

7. **Puebco's recycled rubber bucket,** composed of old shoe soles, for soaking hand washables; puebco.us.

8. **Wool dryer balls** by Moss Creek Wool Works, for more efficient machine drying. They have a life span of five hundred loads and can be composted; danslesac.co.

9. **Cherrywood washboards,** in two sizes, by Tosaryu: good for removing stains and hand-washing undergarments; jinenstore.com.

10. **La Conner laundry soaps,** free of fillers, parabens, phosphates, chlorine, and artificial colors or fragrances, and sold in glass jars; handmadelaconner.com.

11. **Meliora laundry soaps** packaged in recyclable cardboard and steel canisters, with refills available in compostable paper bags; meliorameansbetter.com.

12. **Marius Fabre Marseille soap,** made from 100 percent vegetable oils, for hand-washing laundry; marius-fabre.com.

13. **Coconut oil–based stain sticks** by Celsious (top) and SoulShine Soap Company (bottom); celsious.com and soulshinesoapcompany.com.

14. **IKEA 365+ glass jar and lid,** sized right for filling with laundry soap; ikea.com.

15. **Clothing brushes** for freshening up your wardrobe between washings. The round kilned ash examples—with soft bristles to counter pilling and stiff ones for fiber care—are by Tangent GC; the rectangular walnut suit brush is by Shoji Works; sweetbellausa.com.

16. **French wicker laundry basket;** flotsamandfork.com.

17. **Cotton mesh bag for delicates,** as an alternative to polyester. This is an Earthling Co. unbleached produce bag. We also recommend Echoview Fiber Mill's cotton laundry bag with metal snaps; theearthlingco.com and echoviewnc.com.

18. **Guppyfriend washing bag,** used to capture microplastics when you machine-wash synthetic clothing; guppyfriend.us.

19. **Tailor's shears and other sewing supplies;** merchantandmills.com and alabamachanin.com.

1

2

3

4

5

6

7

8

9 washboard

10

11 MELIORA

12

13

14

15

16

17 STOP! MICRO

18

19 PINS

The Low-Impact Bedroom

Your bedroom should be a sanctuary, the space where you feel safest and most at ease. Yet for so many, the room ends up being a catchall for clutter. Remodelista editor Justine Hand—a perennially busy mother, photographer, artist, and DIYer (see her projects beginning on page 274)—stripped her and her husband Chad's bedroom in Newton, Massachusetts, to just the necessities, in natural materials only, to create a clean, serene environment for restful pursuits like reading, lounging, and sleeping.

1. **Nontoxic limewash has a lot going for it.** Inspired by the limewash in old New England houses, Justine chose the finish for its chalky texture, healthy creds (among other benefits, it's ideal for allergy sufferers), and ready-to-mix formula: made of crushed limestone and natural pigments, it comes in powdered form—Justine's is from Kalklitir (see more on page 321).

2. **Add exterior storm windows.** When it comes to energy conservation, they can have a comparable effect to replacing old windows with new ones. Justine loved the character of the windows in her 1865 home, so she opted to retrofit them rather than replace them. (For more on retrofitting and replacing windows, see page 297.)

3. **Ban synthetic fibers.** Justine makes her bed with breathable, long-lasting fibers, including a wool comforter from Sonoma Wool Company, a linen duvet cover from Rough Linen, organic cotton sheets from Area, a Citizenry lumbar pillow, and a mohair throw from Evangeline.

4. **Get your sleep secondhand.** The key pieces in this room are used: the canopy bed is an old IKEA design sourced from Craigslist, and the dresser and nightstand are hand-me-downs (Justine gave the nightstand a coat of paint for an easy update). The only new piece of furniture: the wood chair, designed by her friend Deborah Ehrlich (see Deborah's home on page 61).

5. **Go analog.** Technology has streamlined our lives in so many ways, but it can also complicate things. The bedroom is one place where we should feel good about banishing it. Keep your nightstand free of cords and blinking lights and instead find ways to bring beauty and peace bedside. Books, a journal and pen, and fresh-cut flowers are all better than a buzzing phone.

Strategies to Steal

Clean Up the Floor

No off-gassing carpeting here. The natural wool rug is from Hook & Loom, an eco-conscious flooring company in nearby Lenox, Massachusetts. It's undyed, chemical-free, and hand-loomed—meaning no VOC-emitting synthetic backing. (See page 322 for more rug brands we like.)

Build a Better Bed

When shopping for something you'll be lying on for approximately three thousand hours a year, there are some key things to ponder: What is it made of? How is it made? What feels comfortable to you? What might its afterlife look like? (Is it composed of reusable and recyclable parts?) This mattress by Naturepedic is made of organic wool batting and organic latex, with no flame retardants or adhesives. A wool mattress topper from Sonoma Wool Company adds an extra layer of softness (wool is naturally resistant to dust mites, mold, and mildew). And the pillow, from Avocado, is filled with kapok; on top is a homemade pine-needle sachet.

Corral Your Cords

Find a spot far from your bed to charge your smartphone. Even better: use a charging pad, like this one by Courant, from Acacia in San Francisco, which also includes an integrated tray for storing items like jewelry, loose change, and keys.

Upcycle Your Old Sheets

Threadbare or stained sheets cluttering your shelves? Justine found a great new function for them: as *furoshiki*-style bedding bags. She uses an old flat sheet to wrap up seasonal bedding for storage.

Who is she? The Hudson Valley–based author of *Make Thrift Mend* and *Mending Matters*, Katrina Rodabaugh is known for her creative use of needle and thread. (Her Instagram account is chock-full of inspired ways to mend and patch clothing that has seen better days.) "The most sustainable clothes are the ones we already own," notes the slow fashion advocate. "But I don't think of sustainable fashion as deprivation so much as opportunity. I see it as a creative practice."

Katrina Rodabaugh

How can we all make better, more mindful wardrobe choices?

1. Treat your clothing with TLC. "Tend to garments with care: mend them as soon as you notice a tear or hole. If you're willing to mend an item, you're probably willing to mend it again because you've already made an investment of time," says Katrina, who also advocates gentle laundering practices such as washing with cold water and air-drying.

2. Consider other options before you donate. Giving unwanted clothing to charities isn't the most eco-friendly option, Katrina warns, because "surplus donations often end up in landfills or shipped overseas, where they disrupt local textile markets." Instead, Katrina finds new uses for her old pieces. "I treat my clothes as source material that can later be dyed with plants or otherwise altered. I often turn clothes into patchwork totes, pouches, and even stuffing for throw pillows." (For easy DIY projects using scrap fabric, see page 278.) Other ideas: host a clothing swap, gift to friends, or sell (chances are, there's a resale shop near you).

3. Commit to slow fashion. "So often folks want to buy a sustainable wardrobe overnight, but that's not truly sustainable. The key to slow fashion is the 'slow' part: to slow down impulse shopping, slow down consumption, and slow down discarding, too. Get clear on your priorities in supporting small, ethical brands, and make that your value in new purchases."

4. Use a decision tree when you're shopping. To make wiser fashion choices, Katrina suggests asking yourself these three questions: (1) Can I instead repair or alter an item of clothing I already own? (2) If not, can I buy a replacement secondhand? (3) If not, can I buy the item from an ethical brand?

5. Choose style over fashion. "Trends shift constantly, and you'll be chasing them forever if you aren't mindful."

6. Focus on biodegradable materials. "We won't be on this planet forever, but those plastic sandals will, so let's skip the plastic when possible."

Bedroom Tool Kit
Our Favorite Low-Impact Accessories

1. Organic cotton pajamas made in India by Domi; sleepdomi.com.

2. Linen duvet cover in "smooth natural" from Tricia Rose's Bay Area bedding company, Rough Linen; roughlinen.com.

3. Egyptian cotton pillowcases by Kotn, a certified B-Corp that works directly with small farms in Egypt and Portugal; kotn.com.

4. Stitched linen waffle blanket by Fog Linen; shop-foglinen.com.

5. Cedarwood, a natural moth deterrent, in different shapes and sizes for arraying in your closet and drawers. Replenish from time to time by lightly sanding and applying cedar essential oil; all purchased from sellers on eBay.

6. Wool slippers by Fog Linen, sewn from wool and linen remnants, with soles made from layers of quilted fabric; shop-foglinen.com.

7. Organic cotton sheets by Coyuchi. The Northern California organic bedding company mends and resells its textiles via a take-back program in partnership with the Renewal Workshop; coyuchi.com.

8. Tray, made from FSC-certified wood harvested in Guatemala, by social enterprise company Itza Wood; bloomist.com.

9. Carafe and tumbler, handblown in Morocco from recycled glass; elsiegreen.com.

10. Stoneware olive pot, repurposed as a jewelry dish; marklewisinteriordesign.com.

11. Dried lavender, for promoting restfulness and keeping the moths away—far preferable to synthetic home fragrances; aPEARLinTHYME on Etsy.

12. Hand-dyed linen sachets filled with locally sourced lavender, from family-run Bay Area business Ardent Goods; ardentgoods.co.

13. Hot water bottle for warmer toes without having to dial up the thermostat. The recyclable bottle by Fashy is from smallflower.com. The knit lambswool cover is by Harriett Grist, who sells her CHICKPEAknit line on Etsy.

14. Purl-knit undyed yak down throw made in Mongolia for Hangai Mountain Textiles. "Yaks graze without uprooting the native steppe grasses like other animals," report Betina and Bill Infante, who launched their line after relocating from Mongolia to Colorado; hangaimountaintextiles.com.

15. Organic bamboo sleep mask that's OEKO-TEX certified (see page 227); simplyorganicbamboo.com.

The Low-Impact Bathroom

Bathrooms come in many styles and sizes, but all are similarly equipped—and take their toll on the environment in the same ways, most notably in terms of water usage. Choosing low-flow fixtures and using water wisely are key to a more sustainable approach. Also important: selecting natural, nontoxic finishes (such as ceramic tiles), accessories, and toiletries. This compact Brooklyn design by architects Bretaigne Walliser and Thom Dalmas of TBo makes eye-opening use of salvaged and recycled materials. It's a spa bath made from cast-offs and filled with ideas worth borrowing. (See two more TBo projects beginning on page 95.)

1. Reclaim your bathtub. This one was an unwanted relic from one of the architects' first clients. It's a cast-iron design made modern with a 4-inch (10-centimeter) cast-in-place concrete topper.

2. A low-flow showerhead is essential—and easy to retrofit to an existing setup. What you want is a model that's earned the EPA's WaterSense label (meaning it uses less than 2 gallons/7.5 liters per minute) but performs well—you shouldn't even notice the difference. Note that bathing daily is a modern American practice that uses 1.2 trillion gallons (4.5 trillion liters) of water annually: as with clothes, you only *need* to wash what needs cleaning. Consider setting up a piping system that collects used shower, bath, and laundry water—aka gray water—for reuse in the garden and yard (for details and resources, see greywateraction.org).

3. A low-flow faucet is also crucial. Choose a model carrying the EPA's WaterSense label, which means it reduces water flow by 30 percent or more. Simple, affordable aerators also decrease splashing and waste—new bath and kitchen faucets come with these; for older models, you can add your own.

4. Go with an eco-friendly shower curtain. This setup is curtain-free, but if your bath needs an enclosure, zero in on one made from a quick-drying natural fiber, preferably linen, hemp, or organic cotton canvas, which can be tossed in the washing machine. If you want a waterproof liner, make sure it's PVC- and BPA-free— Quiet Town is a good source. Note that, in general, water-repellent fabrics are treated with chemicals that are harmful to the environment and should be avoided. Waxed canvas is a notable exception.

5. Turn your bathroom into a nature retreat. Moisture-loving plants, including philodendrons, orchids, and many ferns thrive in humidity. They make an otherwise austere space come alive.

6. Found elements, such as a cinder blocks, can serve as artful shelving.

Strategies to Steal

Build a Sink from Leftovers

The majority of today's bathroom vanities are made from laminate: plastic and particleboard or pressed wood containing glues (and often formaldehyde). A better alternative is to use recycled nontoxic materials, as the architects have done here. This antique marble top is another of their rescues—you can find your own at a salvage yard. They paired it with a Kohler basin and used scrap pine to create a simple stand.

Breathe Easier

Just about all store-bought air fresheners contain hazardous ingredients, including VOCs, and should be avoided. Instead, hang a bundle of eucalyptus: its soothing, nasal passage–clearing fragrance will get activated every time you shower. To further clear the air, use an Energy Star–certified ventilation fan. Turn it on before you get in the shower to prevent the growth of mold and mildew.

Source a Better Towel

Certified organic cotton products are an okay option; even better are the recycled cotton designs slowly becoming more available (see page 212). Also consider less resource-intensive Turkish linen towels and flat-weave cotton towels. In the near future, we predict that hemp and bamboo towels will start to supplant cotton ones. Another recommended (if eyebrow-raising) option: dead stock and secondhand towels—there are a lot out there worth laundering and, yes, using. You'll discover that vintage cotton is thinner than today's fluffy towels but far more absorbent and quicker drying, too.

Flush Less Water

Old toilets use as much as 6 gallons (22.7 liters) per flush—more if your toilet is prone to running. Water-conserving models, by comparison, use 1.28 gallons (4.8 liters) per flush. And a dual-flush model, such as this one from Geberit, also saves water. Extra credit: Install a composting toilet that requires no water. These continue to improve in design and function; building codes in the US, however, typically require on-grid dwellings to have at least one flush toilet connected to a sewer or septic system. If you're not up for replacing your toilet, save water by inserting a partially filled water bottle in the tank, so each flush uses less.

Who is she? Linh Truong opened the Soap Dispensary, Vancouver's first refill station, in 2011, selling eco-friendly beauty, toiletry, and cleaning supplies in bulk and package-free—all in the service of reducing waste. For those who wish to send less to the landfill, she recommends doing a personal waste audit: Keep track of everything you throw away for a week. "This will give you a forensic look at your throwaways," Linh says. "It will surprise you! You will see a real improvement by focusing on changing the things or habits that produce the most waste."

Ask the Expert
Linh Truong

What are the most impactful changes we can make to establish more sustainable beauty and hygiene rituals?

1. Use toilet paper made from 100 percent recycled fibers. "It lowers your impact, and no one really notices the difference," Linh says. "Why are we cutting down carbon-sequestering forests to make single-use paper products? Our forests are one of the tools we have to fight climate change." She recommends the Cascades Moka brand. "It is unbleached, third-party certified, manufactured with 100 percent wind energy, and wrapped only with paper, and it comes in a cardboard box."

2. Better yet: Use a bidet. "It is life-changing. So much more hygienic and, can I add, refreshing. Check out the simple bidet attachments from Tushy, among others, that upgrade standard toilets."

3. Overhaul your dental hygiene routine. Conventional daily tooth cleaning yields a ton of waste. Consider buying toothpaste in refillable jars or tubes, or in tablet form. As for floss, Linh says compostable silk or plant fiber versions are available these days. "Be aware, though, that not all plant fiber flosses are compostable. Some are blended with plastic to give them strength."

4. Ban single-use disposables. Tossable cotton wipes, swabs, razors, sanitary napkins, and tampons should all be given the heave-ho. Washable makeup pads and nonplastic razors are easy to source these days. As for menstrual hygiene, seek out reusable menstrual cups, reusable pads, and period panties. "A $40 menstrual cup can last a woman many years. It is safer than tampons, and with the average woman estimated to use eleven thousand tampons in her lifetime, it can make a huge environmental impact."

5. Make your plastic toothbrush last longer. Bamboo toothbrushes are a good idea, but if you prefer a plastic toothbrush, simply elongate its life. "Many dentists recommend that we replace our toothbrushes every three months or after an illness because they harbor germs in the bristles," says Linh. "You can keep using your toothbrush way longer if you sanitize it regularly by soaking it in mouthwash, hydrogen peroxide, or antibacterial essential oils. I use a potent blend from Uncle Harry's called Four Bandits Anti-Germ. I wet my toothbrush with water and put a few drops of undiluted Four Bandits on my bristles. I leave it for ten to thirty minutes, then rinse."

6. Steer clear of anything that reads like a chemical cocktail. Ditto products labeled "antibacterial" or "antimicrobial" or those that contain ingredients such as triclosan (which is banned in the US but not in Canada and other countries). "The CDC and WHO have stated that regular soap and water are effective against diseases and infections. Not only are triclosan and the like unnecessary, there are also concerns that they can alter hormone regulation in animals, contribute to the development of antibiotic-resistant bacteria, and harm our immune system, plus they are toxic to aquatic life." Check the Environmental Working Group's Skin Deep database (ewg.org/skindeep) for report cards on specific products.

7. Embrace DIY. The internet (including the Soap Dispensary's website) is chock-full of recipes for natural, homemade toothpastes, moisturizers and balms, deodorants, and air fresheners, using ingredients you may already have on hand. "I recommend cross-referencing multiple sites as research, so you can tailor the recipes to your likes and needs."

Bathroom Tool Kit

Our Favorite Low-Impact Accessories

1. Auntie Oti mat-size rag rug, woven in India from scraps of cotton; shop-pod.com and auntieoti.com.

2. Biodegradable dental floss by Public Goods, made of silk with a light coating of plant-based wax and stored in a reusable, refillable glass vial; publicgoods.com.

3. Bamboo toothbrushes with nylon bristles by Goodwell Co. (read about the brand's toothbrush recycling program on page 326). Note that some companies, such as Bite, make bamboo toothbrushes with castor bean oil bristles that can be tossed in a home compost pile; goodwellco.com and bitetoothpastebits.com.

4. Toothpaste (and tooth powder) in a glass jar, like this peppermint oil mineral paste by Georganics, is a good alternative to the kind in a plastic tube—and you can even make your own; georganics.com.

5. Dr. Bronner's castile bar soap in a hinoki dish with removable draining tray by the Kiso Lifestyle Labo; drbronner.com and jinenstore.com.

6. Plant fiber and wood toilet brush and enamelware holder by Utility ("You gotta look at them every day," says designer and Utility owner Martha Tiffin); utilitygreatbritain.co.uk.

7. Hand-knit washcloth made of linen yarn by Mary L. Chan of Bartleby Objects—yes, it's machine washable; bartlebyobjects.com.

8. Reusable face pads by Echoview Fiber Mill have organic cotton flannel on one side and a textured knit on the other; echoviewnc.com.

9. Re.Lana towels by Kontex are composed of 50 percent recycled cotton and 50 percent organic cotton—and are notably soft and light; rikumo.com.

10. Saipua lavender oatmeal soap is made at Sarah Ryhanen's farm, Worlds End, near Albany, New York, from ingredients grown on-site; saipua.com.

11. + 12. By Humankind bar shampoo and conditioner, concentrated and long-lasting. By Humankind soap dishes are made of diatomite, an absorbent sedimentary rock; byhumankind.com.

13. Metal safety razor and eucalyptus shaving soap by Albatross, reusable and appropriate for all shaving needs; albatrossdesigns.it.

14. Agave soap saver bag, for a sudsy scrub that makes use of every scrap. Hang to dry; zerowastestore.com.

15. PlantPaper unbleached tree-free toilet paper, made from FSC-certified bamboo, does the trick and saves paper resources; plantpaper.us.

16. All-wood body brush with detachable bristles that can get soapy, by Shoji Works, specialists in traditional grooming brushes; beautyhabit.com.

17. Hinoki bath mat by Tosaryu, a woodworking shop in Kochi, Japan. When damp, the wood gets fragrant; jinenstore.com.

18. Sea sponge, a natural aquatic organism, grows back when harvested. Air-dry and clean periodically by soaking for 15 minutes in a mix of 2 cups (500 milliliters) water and 2 tablespoons baking soda; farmtogirl.com.

19. + 20. Bürstenhaus Redecker wooden comb and brush, made to last with sustainably harvested beech and tampico bristles; earthhero.com.

The Low-Impact Garden

Your garden may not be as green as you think—especially if you're in pursuit of unnatural perfection. Instead of using store-bought fertilizers, pesticides, and chemical weed killers, follow the example of photographer Sarah Elliott and her husband, Dan Latinsky, an actuary, who chose an organic and sustainable approach to tending their vegetable garden in Hillsdale, New York.

1. A safe, effective way to deer-proof the garden: Instead of buying deer-repellent sprays or putting up a fence, Sarah and Dan built a screened-in 12-foot-high (3.7-meter) structure to keep out the sizable deer population in their area while still allowing in butterflies and bees. The outdoor "room" was inspired by Los Angeles gardening guru Lauri Kranz's signature minimalist enclosures; it's painted in Benjamin Moore's Jade Romanesque.

2. Choose compost over fertilizer. The former is an all-natural, sustainable way of amending your soil to help plants thrive. Compost has long-lasting valuable effects on both soil and plants, while chemical-laced fertilizer can leach into our water system and has only short-term beneficial effects on plants. (See page 181 for more reasons to compost.)

3. Companion plants can keep pests away. Rather than spray toxic pesticides, the couple grows insect-repelling plants alongside their vegetables. They've added nasturtiums to pull aphids away from other plants, and marigolds to deter pests as well as attract pollinators. Cosmos, zinnias, and chamomile are other good additions to edible gardens, providing both color and pest control.

4. Make paths permeable. Gravel is a versatile, inexpensive hardscaping material that allows rainwater to soak into the soil, thus diverting it (and its possible pollutants) from the water system.

5. Less is more when it comes to lawns. Let go of the idea of the perfect lawn (or any lawn at all, for that matter). Other than regular mowing, take the hands-off approach with grass. "We don't bother with a sprinkler system—we don't mind the grass yellowing in the middle of summer. There's also a lot of clover mixed in, which is a bit more drought-tolerant. We really haven't seen the need for fertilizer; we prefer the natural look," says Sarah.

Strategies to Steal

Buy Organic and Heirloom Seeds

When you buy organic seeds, you're supporting organic farms. You may also want to focus on heirloom seeds, which are seeds for nonhybrid plant varieties that have been cultivated for at least fifty years. One of the main advantages of choosing heirloom is that you can collect the seeds from the plant and save them to grow the same variety again. (If you collect seeds from a hybrid, there's no guarantee that they'll grow into the same plant variety.) Sarah and Dan's 'Black Beauty' tomatoes were grown from Baker Creek heirloom seeds.

Start Seeds Without Plastic

Instead of miniature plastic pots or trays for growing seedlings, consider using an ingenious metal soil-block maker like this one, which turns moistened soil into compact freestanding cubes for starting seeds, completely waste-free. You can also buy biodegradable paper seedling pots, or make your own with newsprint (especially easy with a wooden pot maker; see page 222).

Weed by Hand

Ban toxic chemical weed killers from your gardening
arsenal and commit to slow gardening. "One of our
favorite things to do is go out at dusk, after our son falls
asleep, and have some quiet time to weed, inspect,
and harvest. We're out there most evenings for twenty
to thirty minutes; it coincides well with collecting
ingredients for dinner," says Sarah, who notes that
adding a couple of inches (5 centimeters) of compost
at the beginning of the growing season has also helped
keep weeds in check.

Install Drip Irrigation

In the US, outdoor water usage accounts for about
30 percent of a household's water consumption, and
can be as high as 60 percent in drier regions like the
Southwest. One way to conserve water in the garden
is to install a drip irrigation system, which slowly and
efficiently releases water directly to the plant roots,
ensuring proper absorption and less runoff. Sarah and
Dan installed theirs using a DripWorks irrigation kit.

Who is she? Summer Rayne Oakes—yes, that very apt name is what's on her birth certificate—is an environmentalist, author, social media star, model, sustainable fashion advocate, and chicken whisperer. But she's perhaps best known as the self-described "crazy plant lady" who shares her Brooklyn apartment (pictured above) with a thousand houseplants—and, in doing so, has inspired countless others to start their own indoor jungles. Summer has been studying the natural world since childhood and has a degree in environmental science and entomology from Cornell. Find many of her tips in her book *How to Make a Plant Love You* and on her YouTube channels, Plant One on Me and Flock Finger Lakes (a chronicle of her latest project developing a cohousing community on 90 acres/36 hectares in upstate New York).

Summer Rayne Oakes

What's the secret to a thriving indoor garden?

1. Put the plant first. "Ask yourself what type of plants would like to live in your home, as opposed to what plants you want there. When you turn that question around, you immediately begin figuring out what's best for your conditions," says Summer. (Think of this as the indoor version of growing native plants.) "Cacti, succulents, herbs, and light-loving plants love southern exposure. Plants such as begonias, jewel orchids, and prayer plants like north-facing windows, where the light is even and not too bright. Plants that can tolerate less light do well with western exposure's indirect light. And a range of plants will do well on the east side, where they'll get good light throughout the day."

2. Buy direct from nurseries. "Supporting the growers is so important, because we're losing them in this country," says Summer. While she's not above picking up a plant at Home Depot, she's mindful that "plants at home improvement stores are there to bring people into the garden center, where the company can make money selling chemicals for lawn care. It's like the floral section of a supermarket: it's there to supply a feeling of freshness."

3. Prioritize terra-cotta pots. One way to prevent overwatering is to use terra-cotta planters, which are porous and will draw excess water from the soil and retain it. You'll also want to make sure there's a drainage hole at the bottom of the pot and a well-draining growing medium inside.

4. Open a window. That feeling you get when you step outside for some air after being indoors all day? Plants appreciate that, too, Summer says. Like us, they breathe, and airflow is also important for moisture evaporation and preventing rot. (That said, in the winter, she moves cold-averse plants away from drafty windows.)

5. Wait to feed. Houseplants need fertilizer for optimal growth because frequent watering can leach nutrients out of the soil. The key is knowing *when* to fertilize your houseplant. Typically, plants purchased in stores or nurseries already have a slow-release fertilizer mixed into their potting soil. To avoid overfertilizing, Summer recommends waiting at least two months to add more nutrients, then doing so only during the growing season (spring and summer). "When the time comes, I keep it simple: I like a liquid fertilizer, such as those from Espoma, or one that can be dissolved in liquid, so that you can water your plants and fertilize them at the same time."

6. Let them hibernate. Most plants have a dormancy period, when growth comes to a stop and they need less attention, water, and light. If you don't adjust your watering schedule and cut out the fertilizer during this time, you'll disrupt the plant's natural cycle of rest and growth. Research when your plant will be in its dormant state, Summer advises, so you can better care for it.

7. Don't give up—propagate. "A lot of plants have the ability to asexually reproduce, so even when one is in dire straits—for instance, overwatered and suffering from root rot—if there's a part of it that's clean, you can likely propagate it." That's often as easy as sticking a cutting in a glass of water, waiting for the roots to grow, then potting it.

8. Attend a plant swap. It's a wonderful way to start, add to, and/or diversify your collection. Go to plantswap.org to find events near you. Summer's own website, homesteadbrooklyn.com, has a calendar of plant swaps, as well as the step-by-step lowdown on how to organize your own.

Make It Social

Research has shown that being connected to your community is one of the main ingredients of a longer, more fulfilling life. When you share your tools, expertise, and extras of all sorts with others, you're not only deepening and increasing those relationships, you're also saying no to wasteful consumerism.

1. Become a member of a food coop and/ or join a CSA (community-supported agriculture) program.

2. Sign up for a community garden and grow your own herbs and vegetables.

3. Keep an eye out for local plant swaps, the ideal way to offload your extras and acquire new greenery. Plantswap.org is a good starting place.

4. Participate in a "library of things," a lending library stocked with kitchen gadgets, sewing machines, fishing rods, and more—yes, these exist and might even be an offshoot of your local public library (for more details, see page 329).

5. Throw a clothes-swap party with friends to pass on garments, shoes, and accessories that don't work for you—and take home some that do.

6. Attend a sewing bee or knitting "stitch and bitch" and pick up some new skills.

7. Volunteer at a thrift shop that supports a charity you care about (bonus: you'll get first dibs on donated items).

8. Organize a town repair café or fix-it fair, where bike mechanics, woodworkers, sewers, and other amateur doers offer their repair know-how, often for free or for a small donation.

Garden Tool Kit

Our Favorite Low-Impact Accessories

1. **Solar-powered string lights;** shopterrain.com.

2. **Bee house** designed as a place for female mason bees to lay their eggs. Mason bees, known to be superior pollinators, are solitary and, unlike honeybees, don't live in hives; welliveroutdoors.com.

3. **Roosting pockets** made of natural grass fibers, to protect small birds like chickadees, wrens, and finches from the elements; duncraft.com.

4. **Brass rain gauge** to measure both rainfall and the amount of water your garden is getting (helpful for water conservation efforts); rejuvenation.com.

5. **Nutscene twine stand** with jute twine and a base made of oak from managed forests; bloomist.com.

6. **Metal snippers** for cutting herbs and flowers, in a recycled leather pouch; bloomist.com.

7. **Hand broom** made from natural-dyed sorghum bristles; custodian.studio.

8. **Paper pot press** crafted in England from FSC-certified wood, to turn newsprint into biodegradable seedling pots that can be directly planted in the ground; bostongeneralstore.com.

9. **Cedar bat house,** to encourage bats (natural mosquito killers) to come to your property; welliveroutdoors.com.

10. **Organic seeds** from family-owned Botanical Interests; botanicalinterests.com.

11. **Seed library** that holds up to fifty seed packets; garrettwade.com.

12. **Reusable slate labels** for your seedlings and plants. These come with a wax pencil for easy marking and removing of plant names; bloomist.com.

13. **Terra-cotta pots and saucers by Bergs,** Danish designs made in Italy; shopterrain.com.

14. **Flowerpot brush** with a beech handle and palm-fiber bristles; shopterrain.com.

15. **Garden secateurs** with an ash handle and stainless-steel blades, made to last a lifetime; rejuvenation.com.

16. **Hori knife** that can act as a knife, trowel, saw, and weeder, proving less is more; barebonesliving.com.

17. **Scouring block and sharpening stone** by Niwaki, to extend the life of your tools; shopterrain.com.

18. **Citronella incense coil,** a natural mosquito deterrent, by Fredericks & Mae; fredericksandmae.com.

19. **Garden kneeling pad** from Echoview Fiber Mill, made of waxed cotton (using a non-petroleum-based wax) stuffed with a blend of alpaca and wool; echoviewnc.com.

ECO-CONSCIOUS HOUSEHOLD BASICS

A Cheat Sheet

"There are nutrition labels on packaged food, but there's no regulation that manufacturers have to tell us what's in their goods," says Jonsara Ruth, cofounder and design director of the Parsons School of Design Healthy Materials Lab. To help winnow the choices, we've come up with a guide to the fundamentals every home requires, and included the third-party certifications that informed shoppers should be aware of. Do we at Remodelista own nothing but eco-friendly products? Hardly—but we're all wising up and trying to be better consumers as we go. It's a mindset change, and a gradual transition. As writer Margaret Renkl put it, "Dryer balls won't save the world. Saving the world—and by extension the human race—will take a level of political will the likes of which we have not seen before. . . . Which makes it all the more crucial to do our part, however small."

3

Look for These Labels

A Directory of Third-Party Certifications from Trusted Nonprofits

General Seals of Approval

CERTIFIED B CORPORATION

Certified B Corp businesses are committed to using their power to address social and environmental issues. They have passed the B Impact Assessment, which measures a company's consequences for its workers, customers, community, and environment.

CLIMATE NEUTRAL CERTIFIED

Brands carrying this label have calculated their total greenhouse gas emissions over their company's entire history—and offset those emissions by purchasing carbon credits. Part of the certification process is implementing a plan to further offset their carbon footprint.

CRADLE TO CRADLE CERTIFIED

The standard designates goods designed for a circular economy, one that keeps products and materials in continual use. It measures a product's environmental performance across five categories: material health, material reuse, renewable energy and carbon management, water stewardship, and social fairness.

FAIR TRADE CERTIFIED

One of the most widely recognizable labels, Fair Trade certification applies to products, ingredients, and facilities, ensuring that the farmers and workers are fairly treated. The ideal, of course, is full certification. Note that many brands claim to use "fair trade practices" without offering independent verification.

LIVING WAGE CERTIFIED

The Living Wage Network recognizes businesses that pay their employees fairly. Living wages ensure that workers are able to adequately provide for themselves and their families without having to hold multiple jobs.

1% FOR THE PLANET

Businesses that participate in this program have committed to donating at least 1 percent of their annual profits to approved nonprofits focused on environmental conservation, restoration, and protection.

Appliances and Fixtures

ENERGY STAR

The leading US government–backed endorsement for energy efficiency, this label makes it easy for consumers to identify options that will conserve electricity and minimize environmental impact. All Energy Star labels are independently verified by the EPA.

WATERSENSE

Independently verified by the EPA, WaterSense-stamped wares are 30 percent more water efficient than their uncertified counterparts.

Building Materials

DECLARE

A Declare label is a voluntary, self-disclosed ingredient list that details what a building material is made of, including any and all toxic chemicals. It also includes information on a product's assembly location, embodied carbon, and recyclability. Declare labels are not automatically third-party verified, but producers can opt in to receive a third-party screening of their products.

GREENGUARD

This label is applied to products that meet rigorous criteria for chemical emissions. Its highest level of certification, Greenguard Gold, is reserved for goods that produce zero or near-zero emissions. All certified products—including building materials, paints, furniture, electronics, and cleaning products—are rescreened annually for more than ten thousand VOCs.

Household Goods

MADE SAFE

Certified products do not contain ingredients that are detrimental to human or environmental health. In addition to screening for items on its "Red List" (see the inventory of known harmful chemicals at madesafe.org/science/hazard-list), the nonprofit addresses concerns about potential bioaccumulation and toxicity.

SAFER CHOICE

This label is given to household cleaners that meet the EPA's criteria for health and safety. In order for a product to be certified, its ingredients must be reviewed for toxicity (to humans as well as the environment) and performance (it must be as effective as a conventional product of the same type), and its VOC emissions analyzed to ensure safe indoor air quality. Its packaging must also pass the label's requirements for sustainability.

Mattresses

CERTIPUR-US

Polyurethane foam mattresses, while not the most eco-friendly option, are affordable and popular. If you must go this route, be sure that yours bears this certification, which applies only to polyurethane foam mattresses and guarantees that the product doesn't contain formaldehyde, flame retardants, or other harmful chemicals.

GLOBAL ORGANIC LATEX STANDARD (GOLS)

The label to look for on natural latex mattresses, it's found on products with latex that's 95 percent or more organic.

GLOBAL ORGANIC TEXTILE STANDARD (GOTS)

For other types of mattresses, seek out the GOTS stamp of approval (for a full description, see "Textiles").

Paint (and Other VOC-Emitting Products)

GREEN SEAL

Developed in 1989, Green Seal is one of the oldest environmental certifications. It sets standards for a variety of industries, including paint and cleaning products. The label identifies goods that protect human health, reduce pollution and waste, and conserve resources—without compromising performance.

GREEN WISE

Paints bearing this label have been screened for harmful chemicals, including VOCs, formaldehyde, and methylene chloride. In addition to these standards, Green Wise Gold–certified products adhere to California's Section 01350, one of the most stringent health-based standards for paint emissions in the US today.

Rugs

DOUBLE GREEN

This label guarantees that a carpet is made of at least 10 percent post-consumer recycled carpet material in addition to 10 percent of another post-consumer recycled material. The certification was developed by the Carpet America Recovery Effort, or CARE.

GOODWEAVE

This nonprofit is leading the effort to promote quality working conditions and end child labor in the rug industry. The GoodWeave label ensures that a product was made without child, forced, or bonded labor.

GREEN LABEL PLUS

Developed by the Carpets and Rug Institute, the certificate is awarded to carpets, adhesives, and cushions with low chemical emissions. Products undergo an independent testing process that measures their emissions for a variety of harmful chemicals, as well as their total VOC emissions.

Textiles

GLOBAL ORGANIC TEXTILE STANDARD (GOTS)

The leading international label for organic textiles, GOTS certifies textiles that are made with the least possible environmental impact and under good labor conditions. Because it's a global standard, the certification enables consumers to identify textiles that have been responsibly produced, processed, and exported.

OEKO-TEX

OEKO-TEX–certified textile and leather products do not contain harmful chemicals and are manufactured under environmentally conscientious, socially responsible working conditions. The most rigorous of its standards is the OEKO-TEX "Made in Green" label, which ensures that the product was produced following scrupulous standards at every step in the supply chain. The label, however, does not guarantee that a textile is organic—for that, look for the GOTS stamp.

RESPONSIBLE DOWN STANDARD (RDS) CERTIFIED

The ducks and geese involved in down production are often subjected to inhumane treatment like live-plucking. This international standard conducts rigorous evaluations to confirm that these animals are raised humanely.

Wood Furniture

FOREST STEWARDSHIP COUNCIL (FSC)

The group's goal is to encourage sustainable and economically viable management of the world's forests. The FSC stamp of approval is reserved for products that source their wood from forests that have been independently verified to adhere to the organization's strict social and environmental standards. The FSC 100 percent certification is far better than its FSC Mix certification, which is given to goods that use a mix of wood from FSC-certified forests *and* noncertified forests.

Planet-Friendly
Lightbulbs

Enough with the grumbling about their chilly blue light: LED bulbs are the way to go. They use up to 85 percent less energy than their incandescent cousins, saving you hundreds a year on your electric bill. They are long-lasting (up to twenty-five years, compared with the typical one-year life span of incandescent versions), meaning fewer used-up bulbs in the landfill, and unlike CFLs (compact fluorescent lightbulbs), they don't contain mercury. Besides, the color quality of LEDs (this one is by Tala) has been improving for years; read on to learn what to look for.

Zero In On

Color temperature. An LED bulb will never again turn your bedroom into a sterile operating room—if you pay attention to the numbers printed on the box. The key figure to consider isn't necessarily the brightness, which, for LEDs, is measured in lumens (800 lumens is equivalent to 60 watts, 1100 lumens to 75 watts); it's the bulb's color temperature, measured on the Kelvin (K) scale. The lower the number, the warmer the light: For fail-proof warm ambient light for a living room or bedroom, opt for bulbs in the 2700K range. For a kitchen or work area, 3000K is just right. In addition, there's one more critical value to factor in: the CRI (color rendering index), which describes the quality of the light. Better bulbs will have this number advertised on the packaging. Aim for a CRI of 90 or above; a CRI of 100 indicates lighting that mimics natural daylight.

Extra Credit

Dimmers. The key to LED lighting is getting a good dimmer, according to lighting designer Charlie Dumais. "It doesn't matter what kind of lightbulb you have; if you have the intensity at 100 percent, it's going to be too bright," he says. Look for "warm dim" bulbs, which mimic incandescent bulbs. If you keep the dimmers at a low level, your bulbs will also last longer—a win-win for your home and the environment.

Check For

The Energy Star label, which guarantees that the product meets the energy efficiency guidelines set by the EPA.

Planet-Friendly
Paint

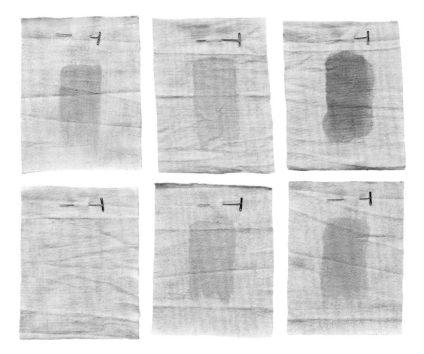

Yes, pay attention to the presence of VOCs (volatile organic compounds) and consider only low- or zero-VOC products. VOCs are emitted as gas and can be harmful to your health; they also play a significant role in the formation of smog and ground-level ozone. But check the ingredients list, too. Water-based latex and acrylic paints, the types most homeowners reach for, are essentially liquid plastic, so while they're better than oil-based paints (a huge off-gassing offender), they're still not particularly eco-friendly. Heeding the advice of the Parsons School of Design Healthy Materials Lab, we recommend selecting wall coverings first on the basis of the binding material used in the mix—and then by color. Bottom-line recommendation: mineral paints (with bases of lime, clay, chalk, and potassium silicate) and linseed paint are far better choices than latex, as are lime- and other naturally derived plasters (which can be tinted, no paint required). For a list of recommended sources, see page 319.

Zero In On

Plant- and mineral-based pigments. In addition to milk paint and limewash, consider chalk, clay, and linseed oil paints; all are excellent nontoxic choices. As with food, the more homegrown the ingredients and the fewer additives present, the better. Also consider skipping paint altogether and opting for unfinished plaster walls. Left in its raw state, plaster is an environmentally sound, breathable material, and it comes in many variations, including Venetian plaster and Moroccan *tadelakt*.

Avoid

Paints labeled "antifungal" or "antimicrobial"; they contain pesticide additives.

Check For

Green Seal GS-11 or Greenguard Gold certification, both of which ensure truly low levels of VOCs (less than 0.42 pounds per gallon/50 grams per liter), as there is currently no industry standard for what "low" means.

Planet-Friendly
Furniture

Think of all the chairs, tables, and sofas that already exist in the world; rather than buy new, seek out secondhand pieces that speak to you—and cost less. And if you *are* buying new, resist the urge to pick up "fast furniture" fabricated on the cheap. Instead, view furnishings as you would real estate: as investments that may well last beyond your lifetime.

Zero In On

Renewable, reclaimed, or recycled materials. When shopping for new furniture, prioritize items made from sustainably harvested wood, salvaged wood (from old furniture or buildings), or recycled metal or plastic. And, as with paint (see page 230), the fewer additives, the better—which means staying away from any upholstered pieces treated with flame-retardant chemicals.

Do or Don't

Particleboard. Engineered woods like particleboard and medium-density fiberboard (MDF) are affordable and easy to find—and, since they're made from recycled wood scraps and sawdust, relatively green. That said, they're not exactly heirloom material. Worse still, most particleboard relies on an adhesive that off-gasses formaldehyde, a potential carcinogen. It's safer to opt for solid wood pieces. Or, if you're buying composite-wood furniture, make sure it's TSCA Title IV compliant; in 2019, the EPA banned all engineered wood products that don't comply with the formaldehyde standards set forth in its Toxic Substances Control Act.

Check For

Wood certified by the FSC, which means it was sourced from a well-managed forest (no clear-cutting allowed). Also seek out the "Cradle to Cradle Certified" label; the global standard verifies that products are made from green materials that can be recycled or reused. Responsible companies (such as Another Country, which made the ensemble shown opposite) have also begun to offer repair, buy-back, and reuse programs for their goods.

Planet-Friendly
Textiles

Shopping for the soft stuff—upholstery, curtains, bedding, napkins—can feel like the fun part of decorating, especially after all the hand-wringing over pricier purchases like sofas and beds. But that doesn't mean you should just pick what's pretty without further thought. As a general rule, the most eco-friendly textiles are recycled or organic.

Zero In On

Organic natural fibers. Organic linen, hemp, bamboo, silk, wool, and cotton are best—the stack shown opposite is Coyuchi's undyed linen chambray. Second best are their nonorganic counterparts, with cotton as a last resort in this category (see stat above). But even nonorganic cotton is better than petroleum-based synthetics like nylon and polyester. Eco-friendly, plant-based synthetic materials like Tencel, lyocell, and modal, however, are acceptable.

Do or Don't

Dyes. Good news if you're a minimalist with a fondness for neutral colors: The greenest decision you can make when it comes to textiles is choosing organic, unbleached, and undyed fibers—which translates to fabrics in shades of flax, cream, and wheat. (Heavy metals and other carcinogens involved in the conventional synthetic dyeing process pollute waterways.) If color is what you're after, though, opt for textiles that use either natural dyes (think indigo or turmeric) or low-impact (aka azo-free) dyes, which are essentially conventional dyes made without many of the toxic chemicals usually involved in the process.

Avoid

Textiles labeled "antimicrobial," "waterproof," or "stain-resistant," as that means they've been doused with harmful ingredients. Also beware of added flame-retardant chemicals.

Check For

Certification from GOTS, which ensures that the product is made from at least 70 percent organic fibers, and from OEKO-TEX, which tests textiles for harmful substances.

Planet-Friendly
Rugs

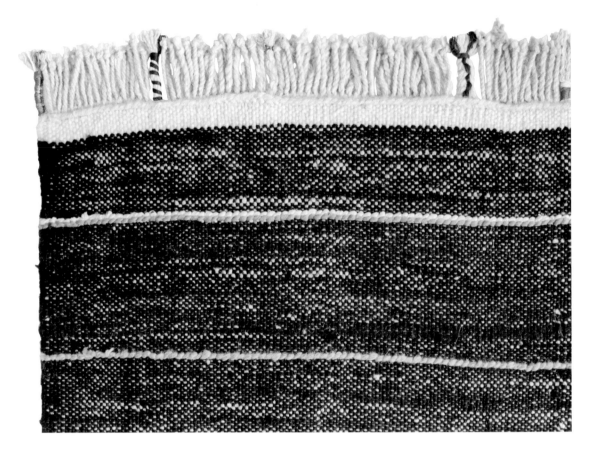

When selecting a rug, ask yourself, Would this floor covering have existed decades ago? For most new rugs, the answer is no: 90 percent of those on the market today are made of nylon or polypropylene, treated with fire retardants, and backed with padding and adhesives, a toxic sandwich of synthetics that has proven to be highly popular, thanks to the affordable pricing. The cost when it comes to the environment and human respiratory health, however, can be significant. That leaves you with the other 10 percent (which is still a lot of good choices): durable natural-fiber designs, including plenty of antique, vintage, and secondhand options.

Zero In On

Well-made designs from eco-friendly
natural materials, such as wool, alpaca,
linen, sisal, jute, abaca, hemp, and cotton
(think rag rugs). The wool kilim pictured
opposite is Hella Jongerius's Argali design.
If the rug requires a pad, go for felt or
natural latex, or use carpet tacks.

Avoid

Rugs created under questionable working
conditions. If the rug was made in a
country where labor regulations are lax,
look for third-party certifications, such as
GoodWeave and SA-8000, that protect
against child labor and advocate for safe
work environments.

Check For

The Greenguard logo or the Carpet and
Rug Institute's Green Label Plus logo (if
you're buying synthetic), both of which
ensure lower VOC emissions. Also inspect
the back of the rug to see how it was
made—irregular knots show it was woven
by hand—and how it was finished.

Who are they? Byron and Dexter Peart are twin brothers who, after working in fashion for two decades, decided to start a company that was antithetical to the trend-dependent, throwaway culture of the industry. Goodee, their rigorously curated housewares and furniture store, launched in 2017 with a focus on ethical, sustainable design and an unusual business strategy: helping consumers "buy *less* but better," says Dexter. "For us, that starts with celebrating things that are built to last, have a minimal-to-zero carbon footprint, and tell a deep and impactful human story."

Ask the Experts
Byron and Dexter Peart

How can we be better-informed, more environmentally conscious consumers?

1. Look for B Corp certifications. Many of the products Goodee carries are stamped with a certification or two (FSC, OEKO-TEX, GOTS, GOLS, etc.), but Byron and Dexter particularly value Certified B Corporations. "We feel it's the leading third-party accreditation for analyzing business activities when it comes to societal and environmental impact," says Dexter. (See page 226 for more information about these certifications from trusted nonprofits.)

2. Lose the buy-use-scrap mentality. Instead, choose wares that can have multiple lives through reuse, repair, and recycling. "Products should support a system that minimizes waste and maximizes the function of each resource. We feel that the greatest impact is achieved when no new virgin resources are needed to create products," says Byron. "For example, we work with a brand called ecoBirdy that makes children's furniture from discarded plastic toys and educates children on recycling."

3. Be wary of greenwashing. A lot of companies offer a green product or two, but a few eco highlights can't make up for their largely profits-over-planet approach. If there's plastic wrap or other unnecessary materials, put the item back.

4. Understand how the product is made. Choosing only natural materials is a great guiding principle when you shop for your home, but go a step further and learn about how those materials are grown and processed. Byron and Dexter are always partial to product development that uses advanced techniques to conserve water and reduce pollution. "We seek out partners that use natural dyeing processes, too," says Byron. In addition, learn if the company is making an effort to reduce its ecological footprint, and how they are going about it; it's a good sign if a product has earned Climate Neutral certification.

5. Don't forget the company's societal footprint. The brothers decided on three pillars when they started Goodee: "Good people, good design, good impact." By "good people," they mean companies that pay fair wages; uplift women; prioritize diversity, equity, and inclusion; and support marginalized communities, often by donating a portion of their profits to their causes. "As Black designers and entrepreneurs ourselves, we recognized early on how undervalued our voices and our creativity were in the sustainability conversation, and we were determined to make a change in the design landscape," says Byron.

6. Educate yourself on the environmental movement. "We strongly believe that most people are well intentioned, but we understand that many find the topic of sustainability overwhelming and daunting. We felt very much the same way ourselves," says Dexter. The twins suggest turning to Intersectional Environmentalist, Parley for the Oceans, Future Earth, and other environmental organizations for news, knowledge, and inspiration.

THE REMODELISTA VINTAGE 75

Favorite Objects for Everyday Use

From potato mashers to measuring tapes, antique (or merely decades-old) everyday household goods are typically better made and more affordable than their brand-new counterparts. Used objects also come with the magic of untold stories, battle scars, and patina, and they don't deplete resources or spread pollution. So we say join the #buynothingnew movement and cherish hand-me-downs and castoffs. Following are seventy-five useful (and plentiful) items: kitchenware, tableware, utilitarian objects, and decor, all easy to find on eBay and Etsy, or at thrift stores and tag sales (see more sourcing tips on page 247). The majority of the designs shown here are from Remodelista editors' own holdings—Justine Hand, Margot Guralnick, and Julie Carlson are our resident collectors—with some loans from relatives and friends. Many are beloved relics from our childhood homes.

4

Kitchenware

1

2

1. Enamelware Dipper

Justine and Margot both grew up with these small pots, useful for melting butter, making Turkish coffee, and heating sauces (or maple syrup for pancakes). Justine sets her dipper in a pot of boiling water to melt wax for making candles.

SOURCE FROM eBay and Etsy, as well as vintage kitchenware and 1960s specialists

SEARCH TERMS "enamelware dipper," "enamelware milk pan," "enamelware butter warmer"

2. Pyrex Measuring Cup

Made of durable, lab-style, heat-resistant tempered glass, this American kitchen icon has been in production—always manufactured in the US—since 1925.

DETAILS WORTH NOTING An indent at the top of the handle serves as a thumb rest, a lasting example of purpose-built design. Older versions have D-shaped handles (as shown here); the open handles on more recent models allow for easy stacking.

3

4

5

3. Enamelware Colander

Early hand-punched metal strainers led to this machine-made enameled version, likely from the 1940s. Cookware with this spatter pattern is known as graniteware.

ENAMELWARE EXPLAINED Enameling is a process in which metal objects are coated with powdered glass and heated at temperatures high enough to melt the glass into a smooth layer that's hygienic and durable.

PRODUCE WASHING TIP Rather than rinsing berries and other small fruit and vegetables in a colander under a running faucet, give them a bath: immerse and swirl them in a bowl of water, then drain in a colander. This uses less water and provides better cleaning.

4. Wooden Spoon

Practical and long-lasting, wooden spoons don't react to acidic ingredients, scratch pots, or heat up quickly—and we know of cooks who are convinced they inherently make food taste better. In recent years, whittling spoons has become a popular craft, bringing a renewed appreciation for hand-carved tools. This lovely example was passed down to Julie by her mother.

5. Ladle

The ladle has been around for thousands of years: early examples were made of gourds and shells. Little was needed to finesse the form, but small improvements over the years include the crooked handle for easy hanging.

"How objects are handed on is all about storytelling. I am giving you this because I love you. Or because it was given to me. Because I bought it somewhere special. Because you will care for it. . . . There is no easy story in legacy."

—Edmund de Waal, *The Hare with Amber Eyes*

6

7

6. Potato Masher

The humble potato masher comes in a range of variations. Some, such as this one, crush the spuds; versions with holes extrude. Both work. How lump-free the results are depends on how much liquid you add and how much gusto you bring to the task.

THE FIRST MASHED POTATOES It's been claimed that the dish is an eighteenth-century French invention, but others say it was a seventeenth-century British discovery resulting from combining potatoes and gravy. The likely winners, however, are the fifteenth-century Incas, who served potatoes every which way.

7. French Wire Salad Basket

An ingenious, multitasking design: carry it to collect your garden greens, run the basket under water to remove dirt, then head back outside, lock the handles, and swing to air-dry your salad. Also useful for gathering eggs.

8. Arabia Enameled Dutch Oven

One of Finland's most-celebrated kitchen- and tableware companies is confusingly named Arabia (after a plot of land in Helsinki where the brand's first factory was built). During the 1950s, '60s, and '70s, Arabia, like fellow Finnish upstart Marimekko, sent its bold, modern designs all over the world. This pot with architectural handles is from Arabia's Finel line (short for "Finland enamel").

8

9

10

11

9. Pyrex Double Boiler
Corning's heatproof glass made its way from industrial use into the kitchen, where it found all sorts of applications. This translucent double boiler, from Corning's Flameware line, can also be used as a saucepan, and is ideal for making rice because you don't have to lift the lid to see the progress.

10. Pastry Cutter
An elemental tool for making piecrusts and biscuits, pastry blenders work by cutting butter into distinct little lumps and blending them into flour—crucial for achieving flakiness (try using your hands, and the butter tragically starts to warm).

11. Ice Cream Scoop
While working at a hotel, Alfred L. Cralle noticed waiters struggling to dole out ice cream. Cralle's solution to the problem, the "Ice Cream Mold and Disher," was patented in 1897 (earning him a place on the not-very-long list of Black inventors recognized for their work in the 1800s). The general shape of the ice cream scoop has remained the same as Cralle conceived it, but there have been so many variations that some industrial design fans just collect scoops. This dipper is by Zeroll, which has been in business since 1935.

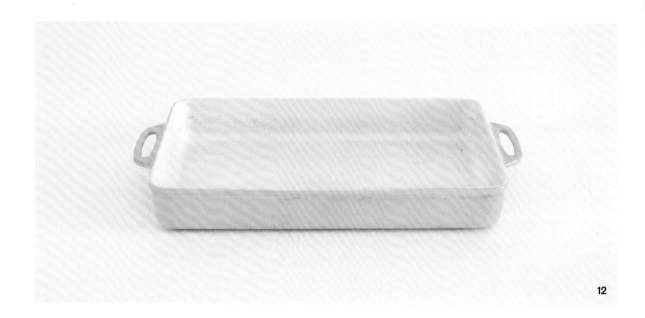

12

13

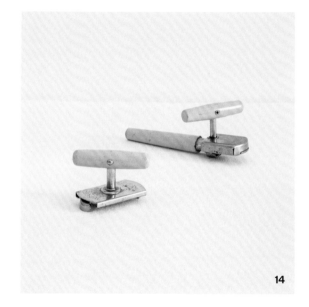

14

12. Dansk Enameled Baking Pan

In the 1950s, a New York couple set out to introduce Scandinavian style to America. Their kitchenware was bright, streamlined, and so high-functioning that it became part of the design landscape for decades. Dansk classics are now in the collections of MoMA, the Smithsonian, and the Louvre. Food52 acquired the company in 2021 with plans to revive the brand.

13. Copco Kettle

There's a reason this kettle looks so familiar: from 1962 through the 1980s, Copco sold more than a million of them, featuring industrial designer Michael Lax's enameled design with its signature bent teak handle.

14. Jar and Can Openers

The can opener as we know it came along in the late 1800s—before that, there was the chisel-and-hammer method. This sunny, mid-century version is much more reliable than its electric counterparts. It's paired with another wood-handled classic, the Top-Off screw-top jar and bottle opener by Edlund Co. of Burlington, Vermont.

15

15. Waring Blender

Fred Waring, a bandleader and radio star who liked to tinker, was one of the first to manufacture an electric "miracle mixer" in the 1930s. Vintage Waring blenders may not be able to crush ice, but they're built to last—we know of an eighty-year-old wedding present that's still making smoothies. This one is the same as the Beehive model from Julie's childhood pantry on Cape Cod.

FUN FACT Jonas Salk used a Waring blender with a special attachment to develop the polio vaccine.

HOW TO FIND A VINTAGE VERSION OF JUST ABOUT ANYTHING

There are the usual, worthwhile places to find old things: your family's cupboards and closets; local resources (moving sales, thrift stores, flea markets, and antiques stores); and online sources (such as eBay and Etsy, as well as Craigslist and Buy Nothing). Here are three additional places you may not have considered.

1. ANTIQUES AND COLLECTIBLES AUCTIONS.

Some of the most avid vintage buyers and real estate stagers we know swear by liveauctioneers .com, a platform for browsing auction sales the world over. Auctionninja.com specializes in auctioning the contents of US households online.

2. ESTATE SALES.

These are best to shop in person: you often get to tour the house, and since everything is being cleared out, you can find that overlooked drawer of 1920s art student drawings. Of late, a lot of local and national estate sales have been taking place online: see estatesales.net, and estatesales.org.

3. AROUND THE NEIGHBORHOOD.

Keep an eye out for your neighbors' discarded treasures (especially the night before garbage pickup). This is especially worthwhile during the spring-cleaning months. Some areas also have bulk-disposal days worth noting. See @stoopingnyc on Instagram for New York City finds.

16

17

18

16. Cast-Iron Skillet

An American stalwart, the cast-iron pan has made a comeback in recent years. Extremely durable, it can go from stovetop to oven, and unlike with a nonstick pan, there's no danger of toxins being emitted when the pan is heated or leaching from a damaged coating.

CARE AND UPKEEP Cast iron lasts forever: even rusty pans can be reconditioned with steel wool and reseasoned with a layer of cooking oil. Treat your pan with care—clean it without soap, oil it as needed, dry it fully before storing—and it will develop a less-stick (if not exactly nonstick) surface.

OLD VS. NEW Early-twentieth-century cast-iron cookware is slightly thinner and smoother than its modern counterparts. This example is a reconditioned 1950s deep skillet/chicken fryer made by Lodge, the oldest family-run foundry in America. (Vintage Griswold, Wagner, and Wapak, all now defunct American makers, have a big following. Unmarked vintage cast-iron pans, such as Lodge's, are just as good and less expensive.)

17. American Stoneware Mixing Bowls

These twin mixing bowls are examples of nineteenth-century farmhouse pottery made in the Midwest, and are perfect for letting dough rise. They remind us of wares made by French pottery Manufacture de Digoin.

SEARCH TERMS "stoneware crock mixing bowl," "yellowware mixing bowl," "salt-glazed mixing bowl"

"The small things of life were often so much bigger than the great things . . . the trivial pleasures like cooking, one's home, little poems especially sad ones, solitary walks, funny things seen and overheard."

—Barbara Pym, *Less Than Angels*

19

18. Perfex Pepper Mill

The 4½-inch-tall (11.4-centimeter) Perfex is the sports car of pepper grinders. Made in Saint-Étienne, France, since 1946, it has a cast-aluminum body and a pull-out chute for easy fill-ups. Adjust the cap screw on the bottom for a coarse or fine grind, courtesy of carbon-steel mechanisms that keep working for a lifetime of use. This one was a splurge by Margot after she overhead a colleague calling it "best in class"—and has been cranking daily for years.

19. Copper Cookware

A culinary status symbol for good reason, copper conducts heat far better than cast iron and stainless steel. Try cooking in a copper saucepan, and you'll be sold. This set belongs to Margot's aunt, who, on her honeymoon in 1964, visited Normandy's Villedieu-les-Poêles, the "city of pots."

CARE AND UPKEEP Most copper cookware is lined with a protective layer of tin that gets worn with use. The pots pictured here have been retinned three times in the past fifty years (search online for a retinner, such as East Coast Tinning). To mix your own polish, dissolve 1 tablespoon salt in ½ cup (120 milliliters) distilled white vinegar. Add enough flour to create a paste.

20

21

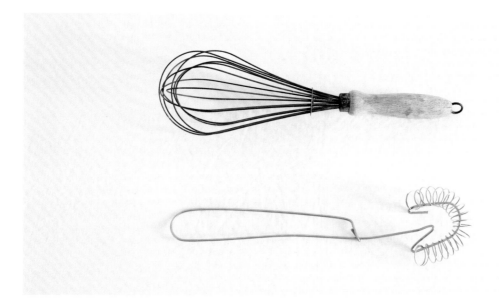

22

20. Egg Beater

In the pre–food processor days, every kitchen had one of these—for scrambling eggs, of course, and also mixing batters and making whipped cream. Search and you'll find a lot of lingering manual-crank egg beaters from the 1940s, '50, and '60s, all with similar features but different proportions and detailing. We like this American-made wood-handled version, and are also fans of balletic-looking French metal beaters.

21. Citrus Juicer

The first of these juicers with "Sunkist" spelled out in raised letters was sold for 16 cents in 1916 as part of the growers' "Drink an Orange" campaign. Made until 1965 (initially in a range of colors, later in white milk glass only), it became America's most produced reamer.

22. Whisks

Americans first learned to make perfectly emulsified vinaigrette by watching Julia Child wield her whisk. Vintage versions, like these two Swedish models, have a certain elegance. The balloon whip belonged to Julie's mother, and the coil whisk came from Justine's great-grandmother.

Traditionally, older folks pass on things of value to the next generation: the family silver, jewelry, Great-Aunt Alma's Hepplewhite dining chairs. Meanwhile, the stuff of daily life—stepladders, clothes hangers, juice glasses—gets dumped in donation boxes without a second thought. But these things stand ready to serve, and when the previous owner was someone dear, that person is with you with every use. As for so-called "brown furniture"—antiques that feel dated and fusty—give them a try. We've seen grandmotherly objects look altogether clean-lined in clutter-free settings. Still too brown? Consider the sacrilege of painting pieces that aren't destined for a museum: a coat or two of color can be transformative.

23

23. Glass Refrigerator Containers

Before Tupperware, there were all-glass "refrigerator dishes," which we've found extremely handy as we attempt post-plastic living. Produced from the 1930s to the 1970s in many shapes, sizes, and colors, they're stackable and ideal for loading with leftovers because you can see the contents. (They're not airtight, though, so if that's a requirement, such as for storing coffee beans, consider a mason jar.) Versions made by Glasbake, Pyrex, and Anchor Hocking (especially their Fire-King line) can be popped in the oven, and unlike so much of the competition, refrigerator containers are perfectly presentable as serving dishes.

SEARCH TERMS "refrigerator dish," "vintage glass refrigerator container"

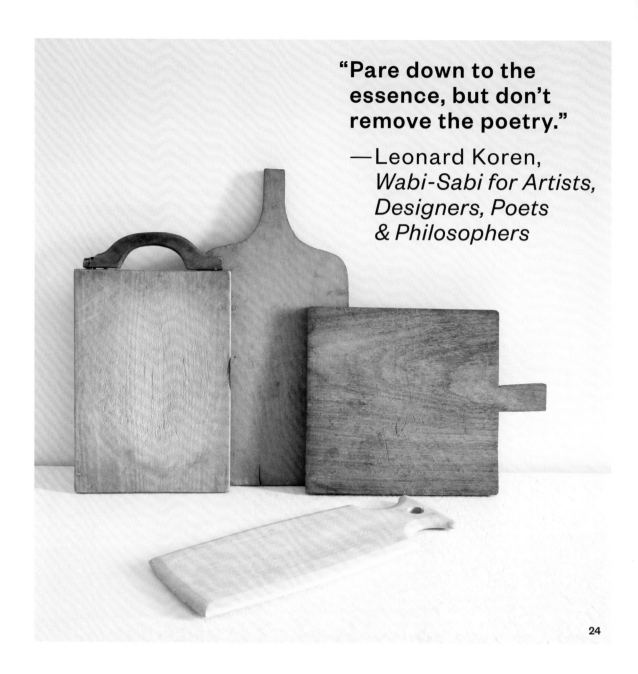

"Pare down to the essence, but don't remove the poetry."

—Leonard Koren,
Wabi-Sabi for Artists, Designers, Poets & Philosophers

24

24. French Wooden Cutting Boards

Kind to knives and long-lasting, the wooden board—for chopping, slicing, and serving—was perfected by the French as usable sculpture.

SOURCE FROM Flea markets in France, eBay, Etsy, and specialty dealers (these are from vintage French home goods purveyor Elsie Green of Concord, California)

CARE AND UPKEEP Sprinkle with coarse salt and scrub with half a lemon. Allow the paste that forms to sit for a few minutes, then rinse, dry thoroughly, and rub with a food-safe finish, such as beeswax paste.

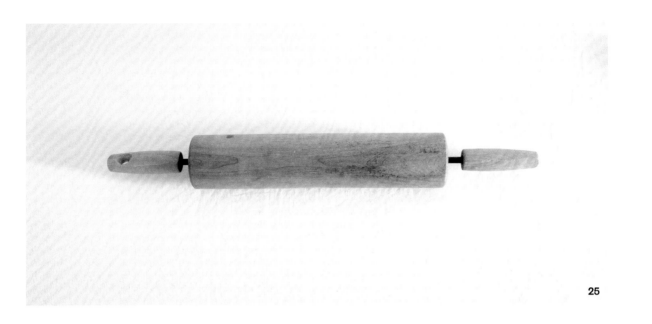

25

26

27

25. Rolling Pin

A kitchen stalwart, the wooden rolling pin remains the tool of choice for rolling out dough of all sorts. Vintage wooden versions are identifiable by the metal center rod connecting handles and pin—similar styles these days have plastic or nylon bearings instead—and a patina acquired from making countless piecrusts.

26. Knife and Sharpener

The carved initials on this stone sharpener are Justine's Grampa Dick's. The knife itself, with its perfect molded handle, is another family hand-me-down, and thanks to the whetstone, is still sharp. Watch Tasty's "How to Sharpen Dull Knives" YouTube tutorial for knife maintenance 101.

27. Tea Towels

The absorbent microfiber cloth is a great surface cleaner but an environmental nightmare: every time these synthetics are laundered, they shed millions of microfibers too small to be filtered that end up wreaking havoc in waterways (for more on this, see page 191). Use vintage cloth tea towels instead. Examples in striped patterns from the 1930s to the 1950s abound, often embellished with the original owners' embroidery. Choose linen for lint-free glass drying and polishing.

28

29

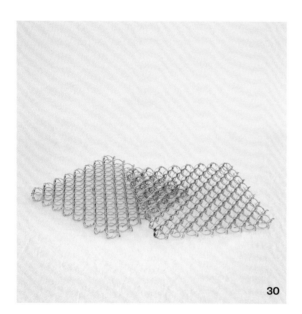

30

31

28. Turned Wood Bowls

Carved wooden bowls evoke Early American and twenty-first-century tables equally, thanks to a revival in the popularity of woodturning. These are vintage pieces that will very likely serve many more generations.

CARE AND UPKEEP Word once had it that wooden salad bowls should only be rinsed and towel dried, hold the soap. But if you use olive oil in your salad dressings, it will eventually lead to a sticky finish—Margot's family learned this the hard way—so wash your bowls with soap as needed. They also benefit from an occasional seasoning with food-grade mineral oil.

29. Enamelware Pitcher

Vintage enamelware is often datable by its palette: this bright orange table pitcher says "1960s." It's one of many workhorse enamelware designs made in Poland and was loaned to us by mid-century collectors Andrea and Charles Rabinovitch.

30. Wire Trivets

In the vast category of vintage hot pads, our vote goes to the Italian woven wire trivet, a utilitarian chain mail–like twisted metal square. They also work as small cooling racks, and can be placed on a stovetop to reduce the heat while warming sauces.

SEARCH TERMS "woven wire trivets," "twisted wire trivets"

Safety standards have changed, so use common sense before putting things like old cribs and high chairs to use. Vintage items may also contain some now known-to-be-harmful materials, most notably mercury (once commonly used in thermometers and clocks) and lead (found in lead crystal glassware as well as some ceramic glazes). The FDA advises using a lead-testing kit, available at hardware stores and online, to check your wares (note that lab testing is more accurate), and recommends not using questionable pieces for cooking, serving, or storing food. We would not, for instance, use the zinc-topped mason jars shown here for canning. That said, most antiques can be lived with and loved.

32

31. Krenit Bowl

"I wanted no unnecessary ornaments or decorations, just a sharp and balanced interplay of form and material," said Danish scientist-designer Herbert Krenchel of his 1953 Krenit bowl. A modern classic with a shiny enameled interior and matte black body, the thin steel vessel was an engineering feat and an international hit: it's represented in many museums, including MoMA. At Remodelista, three of us coincidentally have vintage Krenit bowls with interiors in white (as shown), chartreuse, and robin's-egg blue. Production of the original ceased in 1964 but resumed in 2008 under design firm Normann Copenhagen in an updated series of colors.

32. Mason Jars

New Jersey tinsmith John Landis Mason patented his molded glass jar for home canning in 1858. Though manufacturers the world over have contributed their own versions of the design, to this day, they're collectively known as mason jars. This pair has rustproof zinc screw tops.

QUAINT NO LONGER Thanks to the plastic-free movement and the rise in plant-based cooking and preserving, mason jars have experienced a revival of late. They're handy for making homemade pickles and storing leftovers, among other things.

Tableware

33

33. Danish Modern Flatware from Japan

While shooting our first book, *Remodelista: A Manual for the Considered Home*, we got to spend the day with actress and design aficionado Julianne Moore, photographing her New York kitchen. When she opened a drawer to show off the Japanese modernist flatware she had just bought while filming in Toronto, it gave Margot a new appreciation for her own inherited 1960s made-in-Japan cutlery. You know how that is: when someone likes what you've got, it becomes that much more precious.

SEARCH TERMS "Danish modern flatware Japan"; also "Dansk flatware 1960s" (for a similar design with brown wooden handles)

34. Ceramic Rice Bowls

Sized to hold a serving of rice in a volcanic mound, these bowls are an Etsy discovery of Fan's. They evoke her Chinese American upbringing in Connecticut and are just right for eating her favorite comfort food, congee.

35. Brown Betty Teapot

"The chances are, if I asked you to draw a teapot from memory, you'd think of a shape not too dissimilar from the Brown Betty," says British ceramic designer Ian McIntire. Made of heat-retaining Staffordshire red clay since the early nineteenth century, the simple design is short and stout. The antithesis of prissy bone china, it's a purely rational and much-loved teapot.

34

35

36

37

36. Mid-century Barware

The 1950s were the cocktail's happiest hour, and the remaining shakers and other accoutrements are ready for the next round. The jigger belonged to Justine's grandfather: "Grampa Dick made a drink at exactly 5:30 p.m. every day. He would share his olives with me."

SEARCH TERMS "mid-century cocktail," "mcm cocktail sets," "vintage cocktail shaker," "retro barware"

37. Duralex Gigogne Tumblers

What's your favorite everyday drinking glass? At Remodelista, we tried hard to engage in a debate— except that the bistroware by Duralex of France kept winning hands down. In particular, we like the Gigogne, a charmingly roly-poly tumbler made of nearly indestructible tempered glass that comes in many sizes and stacks easily—the name is French for "nesting." Synonymous with school cafeterias and café vin de table, the glasses have been manufactured in La Chapelle-Saint-Mesmin since 1945.

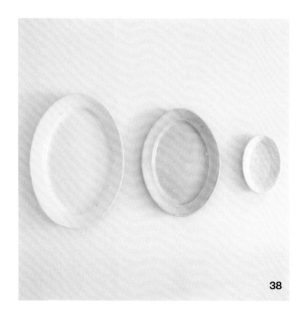

38

39

40

38. White Ironstone Platters

Ironstone was developed in Staffordshire, England, in the early nineteenth century as an everyman's answer to porcelain, and was named to telegraph its durability (it doesn't actually contain any iron). Undecorated white ironstone was a hit in America and was often made expressly for export; by the mid-nineteenth century, production had started in this country, too. Justine assembled this trio one platter at a time; it's but a sampling of her ironstone holdings. "I love the patinas," she says. "They remind me of eggs."

39. Bennington Potters Plates

At Remodelista, we always say white plates are the way to go: they work equally well for everyday meals and special occasions. But some white plates are more notable than others. These, collected by Julie, were made by Bennington Potters of Vermont, stoneware specialists since 1948. They have intentionally wonky edges and come in a subtle white-on-white spatter glazing.

MID-CENTURY HERO The studio was originally a collective, led for decades by David Gil, a Bauhaus-inspired ceramic artist who revived a defunct old New England pottery and applied modernist lines to everyday wares. Bennington Potters is still in business producing its legacy line—with tweaks: these plates now have a uniform silhouette.

1. AT FLEA MARKETS, DO AN INITIAL SWOOP.
Take in the whole show, keeping tabs on the things you're tempted by—snap pictures and take note of booth numbers and prices—while avoiding impulse purchases (unless it's one of a kind or the price is too good to pass up). Look over your finds and ask yourself: "Can I live without this?" If the answer is no, make a beeline back.

2. SEEK AND YOU SHALL FIND.
Sign up for saved searches on eBay and Craigslist. These enable you to receive alerts by email whenever what you're after comes up for sale. It's helpful to be very specific ("1970s black Luxo lamp"), or at least to highlight the details you like ("Victorian beveled mirror" vs. "antique mirror"). Try various descriptions to find the key words that call up the best results. You can also get granular and specify things such as how far you're willing to drive to retrieve an item, whether you want to see new listings only, and your price range.

3. BEWARE SHIPPING COSTS.
When buying larger pieces online, consider limiting your search to your own area, so you can pick up purchases rather than pay for transport, which, of course, comes with its own carbon footprint.

4. DON'T BE AFRAID TO BARTER.
On eBay, a "Best Offer" option indicates that the seller is open to negotiating. And Etsy allows shoppers to query vendors, so if a price seems high, reach out and ask if they can do better. Seasoned antiquers also know that whatever they're after will likely come up for sale again, so rather than overpaying, continue hunting.

5. MAKE THINGS EASY FOR THE SELLER.
People looking to unload goods via classified ads, such as on Craigslist and neighborhood networking site Nextdoor, respond to buyers who let them know they're ready to pay cash, able to pick up the item promptly, and will bring someone along to help with the lugging. (Having a friend with you is also wise for safety; try to arrange daylight meetings in a public setting, such as a grocery store parking lot.)

6. BECOME A REGULAR AT YOUR LOCAL THRIFT SHOP.
The staff will get to know what you're looking for, and, if you're a good customer, will often set aside those items and alert you to come see them.

7. GET IT FOR FREE.
If you're looking to spend as little as possible, keep an eye on your local Buy Nothing group, Facebook Marketplace, and Nextdoor, all of which list local giveaways. On Craigslist, set up a search for "free vintage furniture" or the like. For all, be ready to pounce as soon as something you want comes up. (See more freebie sources on page 324.)

40. Valencia Tableware by Arabia
Proof that a childhood china pattern can impact career choices: By coincidence, several of us at Remodelista grew up with Arabia of Finland's Valencia, the special-occasion tableware hand-painted a potent cobalt blue. Inspired by the traditional ceramics of Southern Europe and Spain, it was produced from 1960 to 1982—and to us, remains timeless and magical. Shown here, a set Justine has been collecting piece by piece.

Decor

41

42

41. Japanese Lacquerware

Lacquerware made from the sap of the urushi tree—also known, fittingly, as the lacquer tree—has been prized for millennia; examples dating from as far back as 5000 BCE have been found. The sap is applied in several coats over wood to create a hard, smooth, waterproof surface. This tray (all but free of ornament, which gives the form prominence) is among the many examples of Japanese lacquerware that have made their way to the US: years ago, it traveled home from Tokyo to Cape Cod with Justine's architect-poet aunt.

42. Mirrors

Versions of looking glasses have been around since antiquity but were rarefied items; most people had to make do with seeing themselves in shiny surfaces and pools of water. Mirrors finally became common household items in the nineteenth century. Now that they're everywhere, we like ours to be old and foxed—for throwing light around a room and casting flattering reflections.

SOURCE FROM Classic side-of-the-road antiques stores and junk shops

43

44

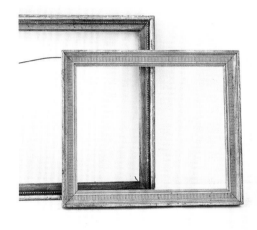

45

43. Camp Blanket

An eighteenth-century trading post staple, Hudson's Bay point blankets were detailed with "points," a system for indicating the blanket's size when folded. Justine got hers, complete with a camper's name label, at the Brimfield Antique Flea Market in Brimfield, Massachusetts.

44. Labware

At Remodelista, we love vintage glass beakers, porcelain evaporating dishes, and other science wares for their poetically practical forms. We use them as vases and for storing things like jewelry and loose change.

SEARCH TERMS "vintage beakers," "antique apothecary glass," "vintage laboratory glass"

45. Repurposed Frames

Frames are pricey when new, and a dime a dozen at secondhand stores. We suggest turning found frames into DIY projects: install screw eyes on the back and string them with wire for hanging. If new glass is needed, you can get a sheet cut to size for very little at a hardware or building supply store (just be warned: the edges are *sharp*). Mats are optional: they're available precut at art supply stores. Trim a piece of cardboard with a craft knife to fit the back—acid-free is ideal, but an old cardboard box also works if you're not framing something precious. To secure the artwork in place, use metal glazier points—available for pennies from art and building supply stores.

"I now kind of see all of these books and objects as being from a library where the loan term is a lifetime, and when you die, your stuff goes back into circulation."
—author and collector Heidi Julavits

46

46. Homespun Textiles

Fabric is a taken-for-granted but crucial element of our lives: we wear it, sleep on it, bundle babies in it. Old textiles, often woven and dyed by hand, have a texture, weight, and palette that distinguish them from their machine-made counterparts. Shown here is a sampling from Justine's collection, which she uses as tablecloths, sofa covers, and picnic blankets. The indigo yardage is from France, and the patterned piece on top is a Japanese furoshiki, used for transporting items like fruit and wrapping gifts.

READ ABOUT IT The journal *Tatter* and its Brooklyn textile library, Blue, are devoted to "considering and celebrating cloth's intrinsic and essential relationship to human life."

47. Swedish Bean Pots

The town of Höganäs is the Staffordshire of Sweden: famous for its ceramics. The salt-glazed stoneware designs from Höganäs Keramik, founded in 1909 and now part of the Finnish design brand Iittala, are identifiable by their simple silhouettes and stamped logos. These bean pots are perfect for storing loose change or hiding a key.

47

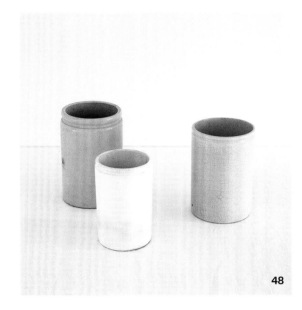

48

49

50

48. Ironstone Mustard Jars

It's a distressing mental leap to compare today's plastic squeeze bottles with the made-to-be-reused ironstone vessels that jams and condiments once came in. We use them as vases, toothbrush holders, and receptacles for flatware and other kitchen tools.

49. Stoneware Bottle

Once the norm for storing beer, ale, and other beverages, stoneware bottles call to mind Giorgio Morandi still lifes. They make excellent vases for a few long stems and can also be converted into table lamps (see page 283).

50. Bentwood and Shaker Boxes

Made for shipping and storing butter and wheels of cheese, bentwood boxes (bottom) are composed of steam-curved wood held together with nails rather than glue. The form was refined by the Shakers into their signature oval design (top), detailed with "swallowtail projections" that allow the wood to expand and shrink without splitting. Produced in a range of sizes, they can store, as the Shakers demonstrated, just about anything, from herbs and other dried goods to sewing notions, nails and screws, and paint pigments.

Utility

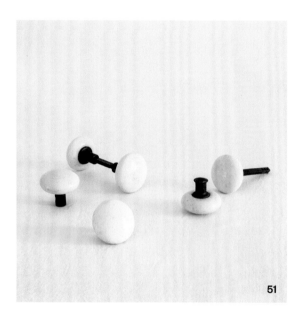

51

52

51. Porcelain Doorknobs

Just as buttons can elevate or drag down the look of a suit, knobs impact the look of a space. And think of how many times a day you put them to work. To install vintage versions, you typically need to add a correctly sized spindle, the axle that connects a pair of knobs (these are available from houseofantiquehardware.com). As is, antique knobs can be used as wall hooks, paperweights, or sculptural objects. Find them for sale by the crateful at barn sales, as well as on eBay and Etsy, sometimes already fitted with the necessary new hardware.

52. Japanese Zokin Cloths

Made from layered fabric scraps, the *zokin* is a Japanese utility cloth used for dusting and cleaning; *zo* means "miscellaneous," and *kin* means "cloth." Collectible ones, such as these quilted versions with sashiko stitching, date from the lean post–World War II era, when worn kimono fabrics and other textiles were artfully repurposed and then patched with use. You can find a steady supply of zokin on Etsy.

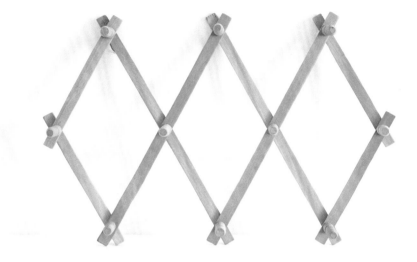

53

54

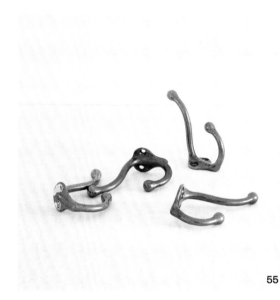

55

53. Accordion Peg Rack

A relative of the Shaker peg rail, accordion racks are perfect for entryways. These unsung storage heroes also work in the kitchen, for organizing mugs and towels; in bedrooms, for keeping often-worn clothes on hand; and in bathrooms, for hanging towels and robes.

54. Dustpan and Brushes

Handmade cleaning tools are hands down nicer to look at and to use than their machine-made counterparts. They're also longer-lasting: this copper dustpan, wooden brush, and straw whisk were saved from utility closets past. The latter is a decades-old example from Berea College (see page 311).

55. Double Coat Hooks

Even the modest, made-to-serve coat hook sometimes comes with a provenance. Julie bought these nickel-plated examples online from Olde Good Things; they were salvaged from New York's Waldorf Astoria hotel. Cole Porter, Elizabeth Taylor, and Frank Sinatra just might have hung their hats on these.

56

57

58

59

56. Stepladder

Every household needs a collapsible mini ladder for reaching top shelves. Vintage wooden versions, such as this street find, also work as plant stands and bare-bones bedside tables.

57. Wooden Step Stool

Even if you have a stool and a stepladder, a step stool is invaluable—for reaching the sink and the kitchen counter if you're small, and just-out-of-reach places for everyone else, such as that top shelf in your closet. Step stools also make good footrests.

58. Laundry Basket

Vote yes on another plastic alternative: the good old laundry basket woven from wicker or wooden slats, such as this New England example with a bentwood rim.

59. Laundry Rack

The clothes dryer didn't become a fixture in American households until the 1960s. Before that, there were outdoor clotheslines and collapsible wooden drying racks. For contemporary counterparts to this one and other options for air-drying, see page 192, and the cedar horse by deVOL pictured on the back cover.

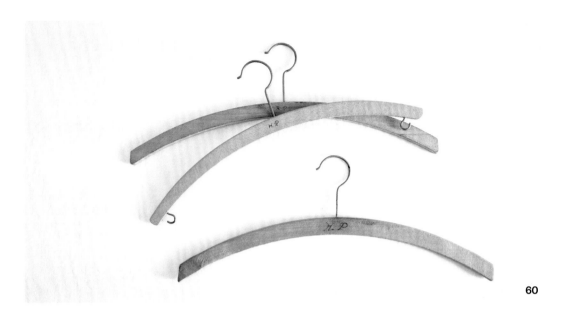

60

61

60. Wooden Clothes Hangers

If you're short on space and looking for something affordable to collect, consider the clothes hangers of yore. Fashioned out of wood and often bearing hotel and dry cleaner logos and telephone numbers (e.g., "Drydock8-1200"), they were thoughtfully detailed to store garments right. And you can put them to use while also admiring your finds: For tidy closets, consider grouping like hangers with like—they hang and slide more evenly that way. Or display your best finds: we know of a couple who installed their collection on a wall as art.

SOURCE FROM eBay and Etsy—both are good places to find sets—as well as thrift stores, rummage sales, and your grandmother's closet.

61. Mini Clip Lights

Made to clamp onto headboards, bedside tables, and books as reading lights, these 1950s designs are appealingly petite and capped with impish mushroom shades. Justine uses hers for "shedding a bit of light in odd places."

SEARCH TERMS "vintage metal clip-on book lamp," "portable bedside clip light"; also include makers' names, such as Leviton, Vuette, and Moviette

62

63

64

62. Wood-Handled Tools

They still make hammers and screwdrivers much like they used to, but without the elegantly shaped and painted wooden handles. And, of course, modern versions lack the tattoos of use. These tools have stuck around—they don't break, so why would you ever buy a new one?

63. Sewing Accessories

Your grandmother sewed all the time. Everyone did— there were buttons to be replaced, pants to hem and patch, socks to darn. Hence all the pincushions, thimbles, and other sewing accoutrements in beguiling colors to be found at flea markets and rummage sales.

64. Trash Receptacles

Even while keeping garbage to a minimum, it's nice to have places on hand to toss throwaways (or store rolls of wallpaper). The good news is there's a wide, wide world of vintage wastebaskets: woven, such as this 1960s Chinese example; schoolhouse metal; DIY crafts projects made from rolled magazine pages; and more.

THINK OUTSIDE THE CAN Vintage buckets also make great wastebaskets.

65

66

65. Luxo Task Lamp

The architect's desk lamp of choice, the Luxo L-1 is a model of industrial chic. Manufactured in Norway by the Luxo company since 1937, the lamp was created by entrepreneur Jac Jacobsen, who was inspired by some springs in a shipment of sewing machines from England—they became the basis for his lamp's exceptional adjustability.

STAR TURN Pixar Animation Studio's mascot, the impish, hopping swivel light, is a nod to cofounder John Lasseter's debut production, the 1986 Oscar-nominated animated short *Luxo Jr.*

66. Household Scissors

An invention nearly as useful as the wheel, two-bladed cutting devices were in use in ancient Mesopotamia. But it wasn't until the mid-eighteenth century in Sheffield, England, that the familiar cast-steel pivot design was developed. Black-handled tailor's shears provided the model for the most popular household scissors. Pictured here are some much-used examples by longtime American makers Wiss and Westcott.

CARE AND UPKEEP To sharpen, remove the center screw. Run the fine side of each blade across a sharpening stone lubricated with oil or water. For more details, watch the tutorial at worksharptools.com.

67

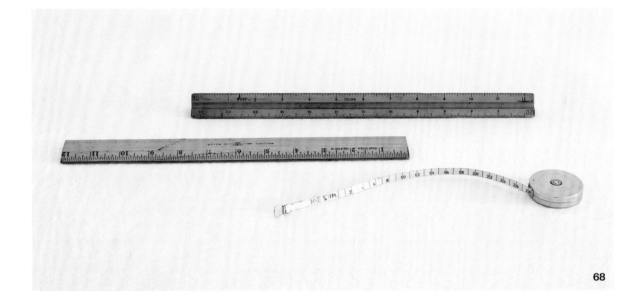

68

67. Ace Pilot Stapler

In 1938, the Ace Fastener Company introduced its eponymous stapler—and continued to produce the same Art Deco meets steampunk design into the 1980s. It's featured in the Made-in-Chicago Museum, which attributes the Pilot's longevity to its high functionality, glamorous silhouette, and "big, shiny knob on top, just asking to be pressed."

68. Wooden Rulers and Retractable Tape Measure

Wooden rulers were once handed out on the first day of elementary school to be used all year, then returned. Retractable tape measures—initially fashioned from the flat wire used for crinoline skirts—became popular Depression-era giveaways for advertising businesses. Which is all to say that there are a lot of vintage measuring tools worth sizing up.

69

70

71

69. Wooden Stool

Use it as a small table, extra seat, or plant stand—or to milk a cow. We love stools for their utility and variety.

70. Chalkboard

The chalkboard may have devolved into a country decorating cliché, but it's hard to resist the elemental real thing, made of slate for marking with chalk, a form of limestone. How to tell an old chalkboard from a new one? Vintage boards are heavy and cold—they're stone, after all—and covered in the ghosts of messages and reminders from days past.

71. Hand-Crank Pencil Sharpener

While electric pencil sharpeners make a horrible shriek and handheld sharpeners are tip breakers, hand-crank sharpeners get the job done right. And they stay put, mounted on a wall or desktop, so you never have to go looking for a knife to whittle a tip. Score one of these for less than $20 on eBay or Etsy.

72

73

74

72. Wire Flower Frogs

An unseen trick of the floral trade, wire frogs are placed at the bottom of vases and bowls to hold stems in place. They've been in use since the sixteenth century in Europe, but the wire and metal ones that we've picked up over the years are from the first half of the twentieth century. We like putting them to use out in the open for propping up branches and dried flowers.

73. Egg Basket

The wire construction of egg baskets allows airflow—so warm eggs can cool—and the openwork bottom keeps the first finds from rolling. Also good for holding potatoes, onions, apples, and just-dug clams and mussels (remove sand by giving the filled bucket a rinse in the ocean).

74. Dansk Garden Tools

Best known for its Nordic-chic tableware (see page 256), Dansk eventually branched into other areas of the home, including the garden. This 1970s trio—a hand fork, trowel, and seedling trowel—are made of rustproof aluminum designed to "feel great in the hand," "support thumb and forefinger," and "reduce wrist fatigue"—all well before everyone knew the term "ergonomic."

75. Canvas Tote

A used indigo canvas bag as a family treasure? Hell, yes. Justine had to battle several relatives to come away with her late aunt Dot's Design Research tote, faded like a pair of old jeans. These are not easy to come by. There are plenty of vintage L.L.Bean boat bags out there, but for worn perfection, you'll have to do some searching.

THE LOW-IMPACT-LIVING PRIMER

Fuss-free DIYs for Household Upkeep and Improvement

Treading lightly on this planet is about learning to be resourceful. When in need of something for your home—whether that's cleaning supplies, a better bureau, or a new light—before buying anything, ask, "Can I make it myself, or mend or otherwise improve what I've already got?" Here's an array of ideas, tips, and truly easy DIYs. These projects by Remodelista editor Justine Hand call for rags, recyclables, and unloved furniture. In other words, they make good use of things you likely have within easy reach.

5

Make Your Own Cleaning Solutions

The dirty secret of store-bought household cleaners is that while they may clean and disinfect the surfaces in your home, they may also be polluting your indoor air with toxic VOCs. The solution: Mix your own. Here are recipes using just four ingredients—distilled white vinegar, baking soda, castile soap, and hydrogen peroxide (the 3 percent version from the drugstore)—for tackling the whole house.

All-Purpose Household Cleaner

Add 1 tablespoon of **castile soap** to 1 cup (250 milliliters) of water in a spray bottle. Shake to combine and use on any surface that can be wiped clean.

All-Purpose Surface Scrub

For extra scouring power, sprinkle **baking soda** onto the dirty surface, then spray it with **all-purpose household cleaner** (see above) to create a paste—and scrub clean. We like keeping baking soda on hand in a mason jar for easy accessibility and presentability.

Disinfectant

Pour **hydrogen peroxide** into a spray bottle and apply it directly to any surface that needs to be disinfected (cutting boards, toilets, doorknobs, the inside of a refrigerator, etc.); let it sit for a few minutes, then rinse. It's a far gentler and more eco-friendly alternative to bleach.

Stainless-Steel Cleaner

Pour undiluted **distilled white vinegar** into a spray bottle and spritz the surface. Using a soft cloth, wipe clean in the direction of the grain (yes, like wood, stainless steel has a grain—on close inspection you can see and feel it). Rinse by wiping down with a cloth dampened with water.

Hardwood Floor Cleaner

Add a drop or two of **castile soap** to 2 cups (500 milliliters) of warm water in a spray bottle. Shake to combine. Spray directly onto the floor and either wipe by hand or mop clean. (Or mix about ¼ cup/60 milliliters of **castile soap** to 2 gallons/ 7.5 liters of warm water if you prefer the cleaner in a bucket.) The same solution can be used for cleaning your kitchen cabinets.

Glass Cleaner

Mix equal parts water and **distilled white vinegar** in a spray bottle. Apply with crumpled newspaper: the fact that newsprint is absorbent and doesn't scratch (and that today's soy-based inks don't run) makes it the perfect answer for streak-free glass, and mirrors, too.

Grout Cleaner

Mix 2 parts **baking soda** to 1 part **hydrogen peroxide**, to create a foamy paste. Layer over grout and use a stiff cleaning brush to scrub clean. For reaching tight spots, an old toothbrush does the trick.

Drain Unclogger

Pour 1 cup (180 grams) of **baking soda** down the drain, then 1 cup (250 milliliters) of **distilled white vinegar**. Wait 5 minutes and follow with 2 cups (500 milliliters) of boiling water to flush. Repeat as needed.

Mineral Deposit Remover

To clear a showerhead or faucet clogged with mineral deposits from hard water, fill a waterproof bag halfway with **distilled white vinegar**. Use a rubber band to tie it around the showerhead or faucet, making sure the gunked-up parts are submerged. Leave it to soak for a couple of hours, then remove the bag and scrub the showerhead or faucet with an old toothbrush.

Laundry Booster

Add 1 cup (250 milliliters) of **hydrogen peroxide** per load to the bleach dispenser of your washing machine to brighten colors and whiten whites. (**Distilled white vinegar** is another effective natural laundry booster; see page 190 for more ideas.)

Give Old Fabric a New Use

Keep a scrap bag for old clothes, sheets, and other fabrics; they will come in handy for so many purposes. Here are a few.

Eco Sponges

Standard kitchen sponges are made of polyurethane, which takes hundreds of years to decompose. Homemade versions stuffed with naturally bacteria-resistant wool are a better alternative. To make one, pin together two 4½-by-6-inch (11.5-by-15-centimeter) rectangles of fabric and sew the edges, leaving an opening to add the stuffing. Turn inside out, stuff with batting (available at sewing stores and online), and stitch closed. Toss in the washing machine to clean.

Wabi-sabi Pot Holders

Reminiscent of those loop pot holders from your elementary school days—
but with a more sophisticated palette, knotty texture, and heft—these
weavings make great use of worn-out jersey cotton. Looms and hooks are
available from craft supply stores; Schylling and Harrisville Designs both
make metal versions. We used a vintage homemade loom—it's easy to
make one yourself from an appropriately sized wooden frame with an even
number of nails on each side.

To create your pot holder, follow the how-to guide that comes with your
loom, or find one online—you can watch videos on YouTube by searching
"loom pot holder tutorial." Rather than using newly purchased loops of
fabric, we worked with long, ¼-inch-wide (6-millimeter) single strips torn
from scraps, tied together and doubled in the weaving process (so they
function like loops). The finished squares work well as pot holders and
trivets, or can be sewn together to make a mat or throw rug.

Scrap Gift Wrap and Ribbons

Bypass wasteful wrapping paper and instead create your own from leftover paper that comes your way as packaging. Rather than tossing it out, smooth, fold, and store it to create a ready supply. Leftover fabric of any sort can be used as wrap, too, or made into homemade ribbons. Here, we used a worn pair of pajama bottoms, a fringed Indian table runner with a big hole in it, and leftovers from a sewing project.

Make your own ribbons by cutting strips of fabric to the desired width and length; for ease and a soft edge, just snip the top of the textile and then rip. The fringe (shown at right, in the center) was created by cutting the edge of a runner and then pairing two lengths of ribbon, so the fringe is on each side. Our brown mesh band (far right) was cut from saved honeycomb paper packaging that came in lieu of Bubble Wrap.

Wrapped Clothes Hangers

An elegant upgrade for basic wire hangers, this project, modeled after the hangers at Pod shop in Cambridge, Massachusetts, is a good way to repurpose torn sheets and pillowcases (we used worn, undyed sheets; stripes and patterns also work well). Wrapping hangers with a layer of fabric adds not only charm but also grip, so clothes are unlikely to slip off. And thanks to their slim profiles, they take up less space than wooden hangers.

Begin by tearing your sheet or other fabric into long 1-inch-wide (2.5-centimeter) strips—snip at the top, then rip. Tie one end of a strip onto the base of the hanger hook and tightly wind the material around the wire. If you run out, simply tie another strip onto the end of the previous one and continue wrapping until you've covered the whole hanger. Finish by knotting the final end at the neck of the hook.

Reinvent Your Recyclables

Embrace circular design—the continual repurposing and reuse of goods and materials—with these easy upgrades for familiar things.

Repurposed Jars with Chalk-Painted Tops

Reuse glass jam, tomato sauce, and other jars. Painting the tops with chalkboard paint adds a pleasing unity and allows you to label each with its contents using chalk. (You may want to prime the lids first; this creates a smoother look and a more durable finish, but the chalk paint will adhere without it.) ECOS Paints makes nontoxic primer and chalkboard paint in a range of colors. Fill the containers with bulk foods, spices, and other kitchen staples.

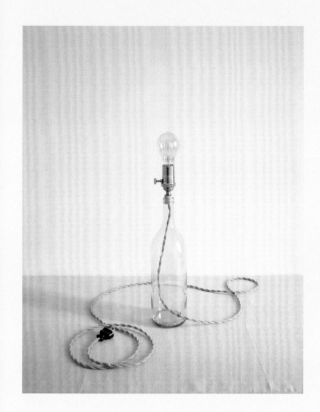

Bottle Lamps

Turn any wine bottle into a one-of-a-kind table light with a DIY lamp kit. You can purchase these from hardware and building supply stores or online (Justine sourced the old-style parts shown here from Etsy seller VintageWire). There are two types to consider: (1) The no-drill, easy version with a cord that runs down the outside of the bottle. This type provides nearly instant gratification and doesn't damage the bottle in any way—but has a slightly less finished look. (2) The drilled-hole option, with the cord threaded inside the bottle.

For the latter, you need an electric drill with a drill bit made for glass (available at any building supply store, typically for between $10 and $20). Search online for a tutorial on how to drill a hole in glass (Bob Vila has a good one). It looks scary, but trust us, it's actually easy, no prior experience necessary. Then run the cord through the hole and out the neck of the bottle. Find another online tutorial to learn how to wire the cord to the socket (again, this is an easy task even for a beginner). Add the bulb (nostalgicbulbs.com has Edison-style LED bulbs, plus vintage-style lamp parts). Finish with the lampshade of your choice—ideally one that's reused—then turn on the light.

Cardboard Drawer Organizers

Have you stopped to admire a well-made cardboard box lately? Rather than breaking down and recycling the small, sturdy boxes made for cell phones and jewelry, put them to work as drawer dividers. You can leave the boxes as is, or spruce them up by lining them with leftover wrapping paper, such as the wood-grain-patterned paper shown here. You can also use wallpaper scraps (see page 288), or the pages from a seed catalog. To add a liner, trace the bottom of the box on the paper, cut it out, and use a thin layer of water-based glue to adhere it to the bottom interior of the box. Leave it at that, or cover the rest of the interior by tracing, cutting, and gluing paper onto each side.

Put a Patch on It

Patching isn't just for your torn denim. Apply the same mending methods to much-used objects around your house, such as fraying upholstery and ripped window screens. Here are some pretty ways to repair holes.

Mended Window Screen

Window screens get a lot of wear and tear. Rather than replacing them—a wasteful and labor-intensive job—consider this quick fix: artful patches fashioned from whatever fabric you have lying around (note that your selection should look good on both sides). This trick, which Justine learned from a friend on Cape Cod, requires only rudimentary sewing skills: Cut a piece of fabric large enough to cover the hole, plus an extra quarter inch (6 millimeters) or so all around; Justine likes to experiment with different shapes. Place it on the inside of the screen, and sew around the edges with a needle and thread.

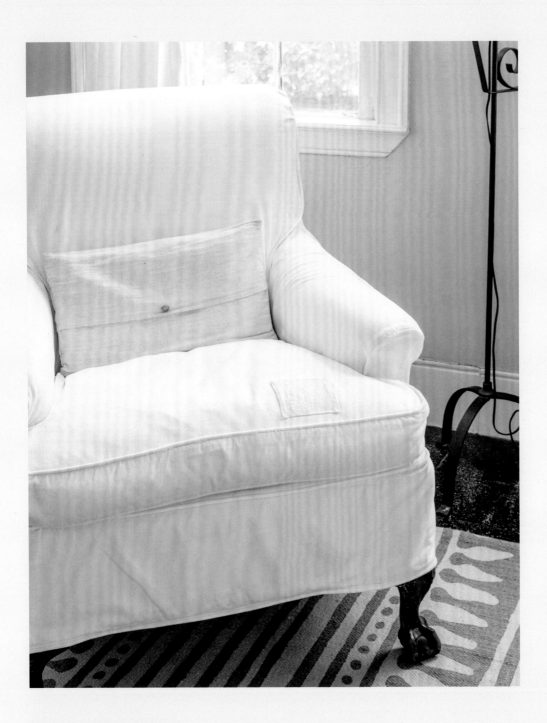

Patched Slipcover

Simple patches are an easy way to extend the life of a torn slipcover or cushion. Note that there are many ways to patch: use a complementary or contrasting color and sew the patch on the outside for a visible mend as we did here (to create a smooth edge, fold under all four sides, iron in place, and trim any bulky corners, if needed); or sew matching fabric on the inside of a hole for a subtler fix. You can also experiment with different kinds of stitching, such as the Japanese geometric embroidery stitch called *sashiko* (which translates as "little stabs").

Upgrade Humble Vintage Pieces

Just because an object has stood the test of time doesn't mean you can't tamper with it. There are plenty of easy ways to make old things more useful and relevant. Staying in circulation, after all, is better than gathering dust.

Hanger Drying Rack

The world is filled with well-made vintage wooden hangers (see page 267 for sourcing information). Add clothespins and string, and a pants hanger becomes a compact drying center for dish towels, socks, gloves, underwear, and other small items. Loop the string around one end of the hanger and wrap three times, then thread with a clothespin, leaving a length of string on each side so the pin hangs at a point. Repeat, evenly spacing the clothespins along the length of the hanger, and neatly tie off the string at the end.

Wallpaper Remnants as Drawer Liners

Wallpaper projects almost always lead to leftovers—some should be saved for patches, but consider using the rest as decorative drawer liners (an idea we borrowed from British interior designer Mark Lewis's kitchens). If you don't have any wallpaper, you can find it in thrift stores, at yard sales, and from myriad sources online.

The old-fashioned practice of lining drawers protects the wood underneath. To flatten rolled wallpaper, cover it with a towel and run an iron over it at low heat. Then cut it to the size of the drawer and use a flat tack in each corner to secure it in place. The block-printed paper shown here, surplus from Margot's front hall, is by Joanna Rock.

Furniture Makeover with Paint

There are many people who consider it a sin to apply paint to wooden furniture. But while it's true that prized antiques lose their value if you modify their finishes, all else is fair game—and a matter of taste. Paint modernizes dated or dull furniture (in this case, an old thrift store bureau with a more recent faux-crackle finish and decals) and highlights its lines and shape.

Before painting, wash the item, sand it with fine- or medium-grit sandpaper (depending on how rough the surface is), and clean off all sawdust. Using the same natural-bristle brush for all the following steps, apply primer, followed by two coats of paint (Justine used Green Planet Paints' plant- and mineral-based AgriPaint in Polar), allowing the first coat to fully dry and cure before starting on the second (the timing for this varies; follow the directions from the paint company). To protect the surface, consider finishing with a coat of linseed oil varnish.

Who is she? Sandra Goldmark is the director of sustainability and climate action at Barnard College, where she teaches theatrical set design, and the author of *Fixation: How to Have Stuff Without Breaking the Planet*. A big-picture thinker, she's also good with her hands: Fixup, her roving New York City pop-up, was an early example of a community-driven repair group, now a global movement. (Find a repair shop near you on repair.org, a valiant organization with a mandate to "fight for your right to fix.")

Ask the Expert
Sandra Goldmark

What are some simple household repairs we should be tackling ourselves?

1. Replace missing buttons. Of course, in order to replace a button, you need to have some buttons on hand, says Sandra: "It's good to keep a little box going; throw any buttons you find in it, drop in the extra buttons that come with new shirts, add some buttons from your mother's attic. Before you know it, you'll have a satisfying collection to run your fingers through." For a basic button-sewing tutorial, check out artofmanliness.com.

2. Mend—don't toss—broken bowls and plates. "You can use five-minute epoxy, the kind that comes in two tubes: Mix, apply with a toothpick, and press the pieces together. A rubber band or two can keep the parts in place while the item dries. You can also use plain old Krazy Glue, especially for more delicate ceramics; white glue is useful for earthenware pots, but it's water-soluble, so don't wash the repaired pots in hot water." Sandra notes that stronger glues have some toxic ingredients and should be used sparingly, but for her, "the impact of a little glue is far less than the impact of making a whole new object."

3. Rewire faulty lamps. "Most often a lamp that won't turn on requires a new socket, new wire, new switch, or all three—it sounds daunting, but this is something you can tackle," Sandra says. "All you really need to do the job is a screwdriver and the replacement parts." She recommends finding a video on YouTube and practicing a few times. (See page 283 for DIY bottle lamps.)

4. Dewobble wooden chairs. This is simple if you get to the problem before it's advanced, says Sandra. "Just inject some wood glue into the joints using a hardware store syringe. Wrap the chair tightly with a ratchet strap or rope or weigh it down with some books to keep the joint pressed firmly in place while the glue dries. This part is crucial, because without pressure, the glue won't bond properly." If the chair really starts falling apart or the dowels break, Sandra concedes, "you might need professional help."

5. Give small appliances periodic checkups. "A little regular care means your machine will be much less likely to wind up in need of an advanced repair," says Sandra. "For example, your coffeemaker may benefit from being descaled once in a while, especially if your water is hard. Just use a mix of white vinegar and water and run your machine through a brew cycle. This will help remove some of the lime and other minerals from the heating element, keeping everything working properly."

EXTRA CREDIT: NEXT-LEVEL FIXES

1. DARN HOLES IN CLOTHES.
"Great for mending sweaters, socks, even jeans, and more durable than patches, because it's a woven repair that's integrated into the item."

2. TROUBLESHOOT YOUR CELL PHONE.
"There are wonderful resources on ifixit.com that will help you tackle your own battery replacements and other common problems."

3. SOLDER METAL.
"Soldering is useful all around the house, from certain lighting and electronics repairs to a wide range of jewelry fixes," she says. Learn how to tackle these by watching YouTube videos, then get yourself a soldering iron.

4. REPLACE A ZIPPER.
Zippers often fail, so it pays to learn how to replace them rather than the entire item. "This requires a sewing machine," says Sandra, "an understanding of zipper sizes and styles, and, admittedly, some patience."

Think Like a Grandmother

Just as Michael Pollan famously came up with the dietary guideline "Don't eat anything your great-grandmother wouldn't recognize as food," we say treat your household goods with the same care that your forebears did—and waste not. Here are seven Depression-era practices that feel all the more relevant today.

1. Save string, aluminum foil, wine corks, wrapping paper—anything reusable. Soap scraps go in a wash bag for the bath (see an example on page 213).

2. Repurpose life's basics. Old toothbrushes as tight-corner scrub brushes, cardboard egg cartons for starting seeds, and jars for food storage. (Shown opposite, pantry items—including burdock vinegar, elderberry shrub, and dried nori—from Severine von Tscharner Fleming's Smithereen Farm in Pembroke, Maine.)

3. Take advantage of dark, cool places as a fridge alternative. Root vegetables and apples keep for months in a cellar, so you'll have a winter supply to go with your jars of preserves.

4. Give worn-out clothes an afterlife—as paper towel alternatives, cleaning cloths, patches, clothes hanger upgrades (see page 281), and more. Keep a collection on hand in a ragbag near your mending pile.

5. Reach for a handkerchief instead of tissues. For full granny mode, tuck it into your sleeve. (Laundering hankies requires water and energy, but in terms of sustainability, that still comes out far ahead of tissues.)

6. Use old-fashioned tricks to adjust the temperature in your house. In the summer, close the shades to keep your rooms cool and add seasonal awnings to the windows, which act like sun hats. In the winter, hang heavy curtains to keep out the cold; a wool "snake" at the bottom of a door or window works as a draft stopper.

7. Wear wool socks to bed, and curl up with a hot water bottle. You'll never be chilly at night again.

THE INNER WORKINGS

Insulation, HVAC, Roofing, and More

Whether you're building or renovating, it pays to learn how to seal up your home as much as possible, and to heat and cool your rooms efficiently. And while the benchmark is a net-zero house (a structure designed to produce as much energy as it needs to heat and cool itself), there are ways to significantly reduce your home's energy consumption and improve air quality without entirely overhauling it. Here's our guide to making better decisions about the unfun fundamentals.

6

Windows

Replacing outdated windows can be costly; to do it right, make sure you're prioritizing durability, planet friendliness, and energy efficiency. Also know that there are good reasons to stick with old windows—as long as you retrofit them to reduce air leakage.

IF YOU'RE LOOKING FOR AN AFFORDABLE APPROACH:

You can have charming old single-paned windows *and* lower energy bills if you mitigate their draftiness with one (or more) of these methods.

1. INSTALL LOW-E STORM WINDOWS. (see right). Paired with your old windows, they're nearly as effective as replacing old windows with double-paned ones.

2. WEATHER-STRIP AND CAULK AIR LEAKS AROUND WINDOWS. Choose Greenguard Gold–certified products.

3. HANG CURTAINS. They can reduce heat loss in the winter and heat gain in the summer. You can go a step further with thermal curtains, which have layers of fabric and batting for extra insulation. Or try insulated cellular shades (also known as honeycomb shades), the best window treatment for maintaining indoor temperature.

4. CONSIDER INTERIOR SHUTTERS AND EXTERIOR AWNINGS AND BLINDS. If you live in a warmer climate, old-fashioned indoor shutters and awnings above your windows help keep the heat at bay. Motorized exterior metal blinds that block the sun before it enters are even more effective.

5. KEEP THE WINDOWS LOCKED. This easy step seals them and prevents significant energy loss.

IF YOU'RE READY FOR A GREEN OVERHAUL:

Go with FSC-certified wood frames, which are renewable and naturally insulating. Fiberglass and composite frames are fine runner-up choices, but know that they're hard to recycle. Whatever you do, avoid buying frames made of vinyl, which are unfortunately the most affordable and popular choice but bad for both humans and the planet.

As for the glazing (glass) itself, the more, the better. Houses built before the 1970s tend to have drafty single-pane windows divided by mullions. Double-glazed windows (which means there are two panes) are good replacement options, but if you can afford to buy triple-glazed, you may want to consider them. The third pane of glass means better energy efficiency (translating to lower energy bills) and also noise reduction. Triple-glazed windows are heavier than double-glazed, so you'll want to check with your contractor or architect to ensure that there's adequate support for them before committing.

In addition to the number of panes, there are two more factors to pay attention to: low-emissivity (Low-E) coatings and added gas insulation. A UV-blocking Low-E coating offers another layer of insulation, as does the addition of nontoxic argon or krypton gas between the panes. So while a triple-glazed window is three times as good as a single-paned window, a triple-glazed window with Low-E and krypton between the panes is five times as good. The Optiwin windows shown opposite in a CO Adaptive Architecture design meet passive house standards (see more on page 307).

CHECK FOR:

The Energy Star label, which certifies that a product has been tested by the National Fenestration Rating Council for air leakage; the window's U-factor (a measure of its heat transfer); and other performance measures. All windows bearing the Energy Star label meet the energy efficiency guidelines set by the EPA.

Sobering Stat
According to the US Department of Energy, 25 to 30 percent of energy used for home heating and cooling is due to heat gain or loss through windows.

Insulation

All insulation is green since it helps keep your home's energy usage low, right? Not exactly. Fiberglass insulation is by far the most popular and affordable option on the market, and while most versions nowadays are formaldehyde-free and made with some percentage of recycled content, the glass fibers can break off and be inhaled, causing lung damage. Consider these more eco-friendly and less harmful alternatives.

IF YOU'RE LOOKING FOR AN AFFORDABLE APPROACH:

You're likely considering spraying foam or blowing loose-fill insulation into a hole cut into the wall. Cellulose insulation (made from recycled paper and newsprint) is an excellent low-impact loose-fill option; mineral wool and cork (in granular form) can also be blown in. As for foam choices, seek out soybean- or castor oil–based spray foam, both of which are less toxic than the standard polyurethane version, which is to be avoided.

Sobering Stat
Most petroleum-based spray foam insulation products use hydrofluorocarbon blowing agents, which have a Global Warming Potential (GWP) that is 1,000 times that of carbon dioxide.

IF YOU'RE READY FOR A GREEN OVERHAUL:

The ideal time to rethink the insulation in your home is if you're embarking on a gut renovation or if you're building from scratch. Consider batts or rolls of hemp, recycled denim, mineral wool (a stone-based mineral fiber), or sheep's wool, all of which are kinder to the planet and humans and insulate just as well as, if not better than, the pink stuff. Insulation made from sheets of cork, one of the most sustainable, natural materials out there, is a great alternative to petroleum-based foam board

insulation, the production of which generates hydrofluorocarbons, which are greenhouse gases. Got stucco or plaster walls? You may want to research using bales of straw for insulation, an old-fashioned method that's enjoying renewed interest.

CHECK FOR:

The Energy Star certification, a Declare list of ingredients, Cradle to Cradle certification, and—if you're thinking of fiberglass options—the Greenguard Gold label. (See page 226 for more on third-party certifications.)

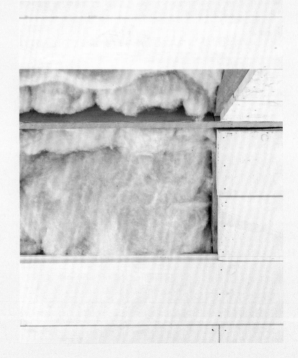

PRO TIP: GET AN ENERGY AUDIT

Hire a qualified technician to do an energy audit of your home. (Many utility companies have someone on staff who can do this.) They will assess your electricity and gas use, use special tools (including an infrared camera) to detect any air leaks, and come up with an action plan for lowering your energy consumption.

HVAC

You can cut your home's environmental footprint by paying close attention to your heating, ventilation, and air-conditioning (HVAC) system. The bottom line: If your system is dated, it can be made more energy efficient. And if you're not currently using green electricity from a renewable resource like solar or wind power, you should work toward that.

IF YOU'RE LOOKING FOR AN AFFORDABLE APPROACH:

Your current system probably consists of a boiler that uses electricity, gas, or oil to heat water that's forced through pipes and radiators to warm your house; or a furnace, which heats air using gas or electricity and blows it through a duct system; and some sort of air-conditioning unit(s). None of these are the best options when it comes to energy efficiency, but there are ways to improve their performance.

- Maintain your HVAC system. That means regular cleaning and replacing filters on furnaces and other parts, or hiring an HVAC professional for annual servicing.

- Install a programmable thermostat (or better yet, a smart thermostat) that gives you more control over your energy use. Set it to modify heating or cooling levels at certain times of day based on your needs.

- If you have older window air conditioners, now is the time to replace them. Freon is one of the worst culprits when it comes to ozone depletion—the EPA banned its use in new models in 2020.

- If you can, swap out window units for a ductless heat pump mini split AC system, which is substantially more energy efficient. A mini split combines an outdoor compressor unit with an air-source heat pump (briefly explained below) and evaporator units mounted on a wall in each room. The heat pump provides cool air in the summer and heat in the winter. The system's price tag is higher than the cost of individual window units, but you'll save money in the long run.

- Consider old-fashioned fans. Adding an attic ventilation fan or a whole-house fan will help cool your rooms in summer by removing stifling air—and save your AC system from working overtime. For added savings, look into a solar-powered fan.

- Replace your old boiler with a condensing boiler. This tankless setup is much more compact than the boilers of yore, saves energy (no hot water sitting in a tank waiting to be used), and has a longer life span.

- Don't forget to button up your house. A surprising amount of energy is lost through windows and doors that don't close properly, as well as uninsulated cellars and attics. Get those sealed to increase your HVAC system's efficiency.

IF YOU'RE READY FOR A GREEN OVERHAUL:

End your reliance on a boiler or furnace to heat your home by installing a heat pump, the latest advance in HVAC. Its promise lies not in new machinery that heats or cools air, but in strategies to move air around your house in energy-saving ways. There are two main heat pump technologies to consider, both fueled by electricity:

- For an air-source heat pump, you install a condenser unit similar to those used for air-conditioning systems in your yard or on a flat roof. Warm and cool air is distributed throughout your home via the existing ductwork—and you no longer need a separate AC system. Air-source heat pumps were once less viable in colder regions, but technological advances have increased their efficiency. However, they're an investment—from $5,000 to as much as $20,000.

- An even more efficient option, a geothermal or ground-source heat pump requires a small well on your property. Whatever the time of year, the temperature just a few feet (about a meter) below the ground's surface remains surprisingly stable. This device takes ground heat and turns it into energy that can be used to warm your home in the winter and cool it in the summer. Though this system is more expensive to install than an air-source heat pump, running you anywhere from $12,000 to $30,000, it can use as much as half the electricity and can cost just pennies to operate. You'll need an expert to determine whether your location is appropriate for a geothermal heat pump.

- If you're building from scratch, consider pairing a heat pump with under-floor radiant heating for the most efficient system. Under-floor heating conducts heat evenly through the floor rather than through the air.

CHECK FOR:

The Energy Star certification, to make sure your new unit is energy efficient. Another rating system is Energy Efficiency Rating (EER, for window ACs) and Seasonal Energy Efficiency Rating (SEER, for central ACs and heat pumps). Products with high ratings can cut your energy use considerably.

Water Heater

Conventional water heaters in American homes consist of a water storage tank powered by either electricity or gas. If yours is close to the end of its ten- to fifteen-year life span, do your homework now and replace it with a more environmentally sound model before it springs a leak. Technological improvements in the past decade have yielded superior versions that will lower both your home's carbon footprint and your energy consumption.

IF YOU'RE LOOKING FOR AN AFFORDABLE APPROACH:

Even if you're not quite ready to commit to a new type of water heater, you can cut down on the energy used to heat water in your home (which typically accounts for up to 18 percent of a home's energy needs): make sure your showerheads and faucets are low-flow and Energy Star–approved models—ditto for your dishwasher and washing machine; choose the shortest wash cycle whenever possible; select cold water for washing your laundry; insulate your water heater; and, when you're on vacation, set it to vacation mode (if yours doesn't have that option, manually lower the temperature to the coolest setting allowed before you leave).

IF YOU'RE READY FOR A GREEN OVERHAUL:

Replace your conventional storage-tank water heater (particularly if it's fueled by gas) with a tankless, solar-powered, or heat-pump version. Note that these alternatives are all more expensive than conventional tank models, but federal, state, and municipal incentives, as well as those offered by utility companies, for converting to a cleaner, more energy-conserving technology, may offset the higher costs.

Tankless models use heat coils to heat water as you need it (as opposed to heating a full tank of water, which requires more energy). This type of on-demand water heater is best for smaller households. Solar water heaters work well for off-grid homes or if you live in a warm, sunny climate; most models have a backup system for colder or cloudy days.

By far the most popular alternative to a conventional water heater, though, is the heat-pump variety (also called a hybrid electric water heater). It leverages the same energy-saving technology as the heat pumps used in HVAC systems and consumes about 60 percent less energy than a conventional water heater. You can buy a heat pump with an integrated storage tank or retrofit your conventional tank with a heat pump. If you already use a geothermal heat pump to heat your home, you can add a part called a desuperheater to heat your water.

CHECK FOR:

The Energy Star label, which guarantees that the product has a high EF (energy factor), a measure of hot water produced per unit of energy consumed.

Sobering Stat
According to the EPA, if all residential electric water heaters in the US were replaced by Energy Star–certified heat-pump water heaters, annual greenhouse gas emissions would decrease by 140 billion pounds (63.5 billion kilograms), equal to the emissions from more than 13 million vehicles.

Flooring

Just say no to the synthetic stuff—in particular, vinyl (PVC). The petrochemical-based product is considered by most to be the worst offender in the flooring world when it comes to the health of the environment and humans: its manufacturing process releases cancer-causing toxins into the air, and, once installed in the home, it can off-gas VOCs for years. And at the end of its life, it's neither recyclable nor biodegradable.

Now that you know what to avoid, what are some options you can embrace? Thankfully, there are many.

IF YOU'RE LOOKING FOR AN AFFORDABLE APPROACH:

Your ideal flooring may be right under your nose. In old houses, ripping up the existing flooring often reveals real hardwood floors (or salvageable subfloors) lying just beneath. And we can't overstate the power of a few well-placed rugs or a canvas floorcloth for distracting the eye from less-than-ideal flooring. (See page 236 for our guide to rugs.)

IF YOU'RE READY FOR A GREEN OVERHAUL:

Begin by selecting natural materials: hardwood, ceramic tiles, linoleum, stone, cork, and bamboo are all durable, good-looking, low-impact options. Engineered hardwood, which is more eco-friendly and attractive than laminate flooring (second only to vinyl in the bad-for-the-environment department), is also okay, as long as formaldehyde isn't among the ingredients.

If hardwood is what you're after, the most sustainable decision you can make is to use salvaged wood (architectural salvage and other specialist companies sell it; see a list of some on page 312). If that's not a possibility, make sure your flooring is FSC certified, which guarantees that it's from a well-managed forest. And, as always, do your best to source locally. It's even more important to buy regionally when it comes to stone flooring, as transporting the heavy material carries a large carbon footprint.

CHECK FOR:

FSC certification if you're looking at new hardwood floors. And choose a natural wood finish like linseed, tung, or hemp oils; if you must go with a polyurethane finish, make sure it's water based and has Green Seal's GS-11 label.

Roofing

When it comes to roofing, it's not easy being green: the eco-friendlier options tend to be the priciest. On the other hand, most of those choices have the longest life span, so an investment now will save you money in the long run—especially since a new energy-efficient roof will reduce your home's heating and cooling bills.

IF YOU HAVE A PITCHED ROOF:

All roofing materials have pros and cons, but the architect's hands-down top choice is standing seam metal, which has a tidy look, requires little or no maintenance, and lasts for decades (say, fifty-plus years for steel and aluminum, a hundred years for zinc and copper). It reflects sunlight and heat, reducing energy costs, and often contains recycled metal (as much as 60 percent). And at the end of its life span, it can be fully recycled. (The example shown here is by Whispering Smith; see pages 113–123.)

Terra-cotta tiles and cedar shingles/shakes are also great options. Both are good insulators and are made from renewable resources. If you're looking into a cedar roof, just be sure the wood is from a responsible source. You may also want to consider synthetic shingles: companies like EcoStar and Enviroshake are recycling some of the 246 million car tires discarded in the US every year into shingles that resemble slate or cedar shakes. These roofs come with a fifty-year warranty.

A note about slate tiles: While a slate roof is durable (it may outlast your house), slate is not a renewable resource nor is it typically recycled for other uses when its job as a roof is done. If you already have a slate roof, you don't need to do much to keep it in good shape. But if you're thinking about installing one, consider other options.

IF YOU HAVE A FLAT ROOF:

Sustainable products for no-slope roofs are, unfortunately, limited. A metal roof is a reliable choice, for the reasons outlined earlier, but most other options rely on synthetic membranes that come with environmental concerns. Whatever you choose, consider making it a "cool roof" by having it coated with pigments that reflect light (and thus heat). Such roofs not only help reduce the effect of "heat islands" but can also lower your energy bill.

Or install a "living roof," which may be the greenest option of all. These roofs add vegetation to an urban landscape, reduce rainwater runoff (meaning fewer pollutants enter the water supply), and cut heating and cooling costs. If you're DIYing a green roof, make sure to use a water- and root-proof liner and to choose a lightweight growing medium and low- or no-maintenance plants. Sedum mats made specifically for green roofs can help simplify the installation process. Green roofs do require maintenance (less over time), but can last up to fifty years. Note that your roof must be well supported, as the weight of a roof filled with soil and plants can be considerable. And, of course, reliable sun is a must.

HARNESSING THE SUN: WHAT YOU NEED TO KNOW ABOUT SOLAR PANELS

Over the years, fossil fuels—natural gas, coal, and oil—have generated much of the energy used around the world, polluting the air and adding to the buildup of greenhouse gases in the atmosphere. But sunshine is a plentiful, nonpolluting resource, and it's free. Prices for solar panels have dropped, and after federal tax credits and state rebates, installing them might run around $12,500 for the average house. Depending on a number of factors (such as climate, location, and household energy requirements), you can recoup the cost, on average, in eight years, and from there, save thousands on your electric bill over the life span of your solar setup (about twenty-five years). What's more, solar roof panels increase the value of your house.

You'll want to find a solar energy company you trust for a professional consultation and installation. Two well-rated businesses to look into are Vivint Solar and Tesla—yes, *that* Tesla.

Note that not all solar panels are the same: some buyers prefer the glossy black surface of monocrystalline silicon panels, which are the most efficient and most expensive, over the variegated blue finish of polycrystalline silicon panels. Don't like the look of solar panels on a roof? You can also mount them on the ground. Or consider joining a local solar project invested in bringing renewable power to your community.

The building industry needs to mend its materials and ways. Turn to these websites for eco-minded intel on the many elements that go into home-building and remodeling projects. (Shown opposite: clay-plastered walls in Susann Probst and Yannic Schon's thoughtfully remodeled attic studio; see their garden on pages 164–171.)

ARCHITECTURE 2030

architecture2030.org/palette

"To make all new buildings and renovations carbon-neutral by the year 2030" is the mission of this international nonprofit. Their 2030 Palette offers an in-depth look at sustainable strategies and materials for insulation, drywall, anything made of wood, and more. Also see its reports on using straw bales, sheep's wool, and other "carbon smart materials."

BUILDINGGREEN

buildinggreen.com

A long-standing, trusted industry resource, BuildingGreen offers the latest news and information on sustainable construction practices, materials, and products. Caveat: Most BuildingGreen content is available only to members or for a fee, but monthly subscriptions are an option.

ENERGY.GOV

The US Department of Energy's consumer information bank covers all aspects of the energy-efficient home, from how to perform a DIY home energy audit to HVAC systems guidance.

THE ENVIRONMENTAL WORKING GROUP'S HEALTHY LIVING: HOME GUIDE

ewg.org/healthyhomeguide

A nonprofit activist group, the EWG specializes in doing research that allows consumers to make healthier, more informed choices. In addition to Skin Deep, its well-known cosmetics database, EWG has the Healthy Living: Home Guide to aid buyers in choosing nontoxic materials, furnishings, and systems for every room.

FERNWOOD RENO

netzerovictoria.com

An American couple's adventures assembling a team and converting a historic bungalow in Victoria, Canada, into an energy-neutral dwelling. Wanting to empower others, they share their research and resources on their website and blog.

HBN HEALTHY BUILDING NETWORK

healthybuilding.net

A nonprofit with a focus on "improving hazardous chemical transparency and inspiring product innovation." HBN's HomeFree initiative provides online spec sheets that offer great general guidance on what to look for when choosing sealants, water pipes, countertops, doors, paint, and more.

PARSONS HEALTHY MATERIALS LEARNING HUB

healthymaterialslab.org

The Parsons School of Design's Healthy Materials Lab is a research lab and teaching group "dedicated to a world in which people's health is placed at the center of all design decisions." Look to its Donghia Healthier Materials Library for an online collection of building materials guides as well as links to kindred organizations.

Sobering Stat
Studies show that an uninsulated attic can result in up to 25 percent heat loss.

Who are they? Ruth Mandl and Bobby Johnston's Brooklyn architecture firm, CO Adaptive, specializes in environmentally responsible, future-resilient retrofits (their own kitchen is pictured on pages 174 and 179). The couple converted their 1889 Bed-Stuy brownstone into a passive house by following a set of building standards for ultra-energy efficiency—their power bills are literally zero, electric-car-charging included, and their indoor temperature is steady year-round. The gut renovation required to achieve these standards is not an option for many, but there are elements to their approach that any homeowner can adopt.

Ruth Mandl and Bobby Johnston

What are some green architecture approaches we should be considering for our homes?

1. Add exterior shading to all your windows and glass doors.
The couple's house has motorized exterior metal blinds by Hella that raise, lower, and angle at the press of a button to allow in or keep out the sun, and when fully retracted, are hidden from view. "This small addition blocks solar heat transfer, significantly reducing your cooling demand."

2. Make your roof work harder.
"If your house has the correct orientation and exposure, solar panels are an effective way to offset your energy consumption," notes Ruth. "Where solar panels aren't feasible, green roofs are a sustainable alternative that minimizes stormwater runoff, increases building insulation, and enhances local ecosystems."

3. Upgrade your insulation.
"We have a no-foam rule in our office for two main reasons: the high environmental impact of foam production and installation, as well as its negative impacts on indoor air quality," says Bobby. Fortunately, there are many alternatives that the couple likes, including "blown-in cellulose, sheep's wool insulation, mineral wool insulation, cork, and hempcrete." In their town house, the architects expanded the depth of their front wall by a foot for extra insulation and used blown-in cellulose alongside mineral wool batts.

4. Install high-performance windows.
"When upgrading windows, consider triple-paned windows with gaskets that seal like airplane doors. This will improve the overall airtightness of your house as well as sound isolation from exterior noise," says Ruth. The operation of conventional double-hung windows, she points out, "results in a gap between the panes, allowing air to leak through and creating that drafty feeling. We recommend tilt-and-turn windows, which create a tight seal around the perimeter and allow for a variety of open positions."

5. Move toward renewable energy.
When upgrading existing space heating, water heating, cooking, or other household systems, consider moving away from oil and gas and switching to electricity from a clean source: solar, wind, geothermal, or a combination. "It's the only way we'll be able to holistically offset our energy use," says Ruth.

EXTRA CREDIT: CREATE A PASSIVE HOUSE

Renovating or building to the passive house standard increases the construction cost by 5 to 10 percent, but, Ruth and Bobby point out, pays off in energy savings over the years. (A caveat: Many passive house construction staples are petroleum-based, but there's an effort afoot to remedy that.) According to Ruth and Bobby, there are three key advantages to the approach.

1. GOING NET ZERO.
"When combined with solar power, a passive house uses only as much energy as the building can produce," says Bobby.

2. IMPROVED AIR QUALITY.
"An airtight building envelope with an energy recovery ventilator (ERV), two elements in all passive houses, makes for much cleaner indoor air, positively impacting allergies and asthma, especially in relation to our deteriorating urban air quality," notes Ruth.

3. SIGNIFICANT MONEY SAVINGS DOWN THE LINE.
"There's little in the way of repair and maintenance, lower or no utility bills, and possible independence from the energy grid," adds Ruth. Get the full details from the Passive House Institute US at phius.org.

RESOURCES

Where to Shop and How to Get Rid of Excess

On the following pages, you'll find our roster of stores and brands that can be counted on to deliver ethically made and eco-conscious products, plus myriad ways to unload unwanted things. Trust us, whether you're looking to free yourself of some possessions or buy greener replacements, you'll want to bookmark this section.

7

Makers and Sellers We Swear By

Hunting for well-designed, thoughtfully made everyday things is a way of life at Remodelista. Finding great-looking, ethically produced goods made from aboveboard materials is especially daunting, so allow us to do the legwork for you. Here, we present a list of key categories for the home, each with a selective roster of workshops, stores, and companies whose products and practices reflect the "low impact" ethos. Enjoy browsing, but buy with care, and before investing in anything new, do an online search to check out what you can find in the secondhand market.

AMERICAN HERITAGE BRANDS

Here are some hometown companies known for their tried-and-true, made-in-the-US wares.

BENNINGTON POTTERS
Bennington, VT
benningtonpotters.com

An under-the-radar, mid-century legacy workshop, Bennington Potters continues to produce founder David Gil's modernist take on New England stoneware, including the original "it" mug from the 1970s, the mod and ergonomic Trigger design. In the "Remodelista Vintage 75," see Bennington's iconic spatter-glazed plates (page 258).

BEREA COLLEGE CRAFT
Berea, KY
bcshoppe.com/student-craft/

The South's first interracial and coed institution, Berea has been tuition-free since its founding in 1855. To help make that possible, students hold campus jobs, including carrying on the area's artisan traditions. Berea brooms, woven blankets, and other creations are sold in the school store and online at reasonable prices.

CHICAGO FAUCETS
chicagofaucets.com

For more than a century, Chicago has been producing faucets built, as the company puts it, "for high-use, high-abuse environments." That includes labs, hospitals, and schools, and also residential settings. Its WaterSense-certified kitchen and bathroom fittings are customizable from a variety of components—see an example in the kitchen on page 21. Two good sources for Chicago products are the chicagofaucetshoppe.com and sinkfactory.com.

HEATH CERAMICS
Sausalito, San Francisco, and Los Angeles, CA
heathceramics.com

Edith and Brian Heath ran their iconic California ceramics studio from 1948 to the start of the twenty-first century. Since then, husband-and-wife owners Robin Petravic and Catherine Bailey have carried the torch, continuing to produce handcrafted tableware and tiles, as well as a range of clean-lined home goods.

JACOB BROMWELL
Markle, IN
jacobbromwell.com

Makers of "domestic Americana"—tin cups, copper flasks, flour sifters, and pie tins—the company, founded by frontier entrepreneur Jacob Bromwell, is among the oldest continually operating in the US. Its prices are steep because its standards are unstinting.

JOHN BOOS & CO.
Effingham, IL
johnboos.com

Synonymous since 1887 with butcher-block tables and "Boos blocks," hefty maple cutting boards with edge-grain construction. The company recycles 95 percent of all raw and scrap materials, and uses the sawdust to heat its kilns.

LODGE CAST IRON
South Pittsburg, TN

lodgecastiron.com

More than 120 years after Joseph Lodge began his foundry, members of his family continue to make skillets and other cast-iron cookware in South Pittsburg, Tennessee. Go to page 248 to see a vintage Lodge pan.

STEELE CANVAS BASKET CORP.
Chelsea, MA

steelecanvas.com

Steele specializes in industrial canvas hampers made for use on construction sites and the transportation of dry goods—as well as for laundry, toys, firewood, and more. The family-owned company has been operating just north of Boston since 1921, and its products, always stenciled with the Steele logo, continue to be entirely fabricated by hand.

SWANS ISLAND COMPANY
Northport and Camden, ME

swansislandcompany.com

Makers of handwoven striped cotton and wool blankets, Swans Island sources much of its fiber from New England farms. The company employs a team of dyers who tint all of the yarn by hand and weavers who work on noisy vintage looms (you can watch them in Swans Island's Northport headquarters).

ARCHITECTURAL SALVAGE

The green movement may claim salvage as its own, but the business of saving and reselling building parts is centuries old—and, as a result, there are places to find reclamation in pretty much every corner of the world. Here is but a sampling. Find a good directory of architectural salvage stores in the US at oldhouseonline.com. Note that these businesses buy and sell (some even trade), and most will come dismantle and "harvest" valuable old house parts.

IRREPLACEABLE ARTIFACTS
New York, NY, and Norwich, CT

irreplaceableartifacts.com

A long-standing New York City supplier of antique brass letter boxes, marble fireplace mantels, and countless other things, Irreplaceable Artifacts has a 500,000-square-foot (464,512-square-meter) warehouse in Norwich, Connecticut.

OHMEGA SALVAGE
Berkeley, CA

ohmegasalvage.com

Vintage glass bricks, plaster ceiling rosettes, tall pine dressers, oak coat-trees—just about anything you're looking for can be found at this Berkeley institution.

OLDE NEW ENGLAND SALVAGE CO.
Bozrah, CT

oldenewenglandsalvage.com

A source for antique beams, paneling, flooring, and much more, Olde New England Salvage Co. also buys and sells period structures, and is expert at taking them down and relocating them.

THE OLD HOUSE PARTS COMPANY
Kennebunk, ME

oldhouseparts.com

Located in an 1872 freight warehouse, Old House Parts not only sells salvage from 1730 to 1930 but also dismantles and moves old barns and houses.

OLD WOOD WORKSHOP
Pomfret Center, CT

oldwoodworkshop.com

Dedicated to "giving old wood new life," this small business stocks wide-board flooring, primarily from the eighteenth and nineteenth centuries, and salvaged beams, boards, and joists.

REBUILDING EXCHANGE
Chicago, IL

rebuildingexchange.org

A nonprofit social enterprise that sells affordable reclaimed building materials in Chicago's Bucktown, the Rebuilding Exchange offers job training and work to people with "barriers to employment."

RETROUVIUS
London, England

retrouvius.com

A beloved resource in London's Kensal Green, Retrouvius operates as both a reclamation business and a design studio specializing in inspired uses of salvage (see the cupboards inset with a band of antique cigar molds on page 310). Husband-and-wife owners Adam Hills and Maria Speake are eloquent advocates for their trade: "Reuse," they say, "is not just relevant today, it is vital."

THE REUSE PEOPLE
Locations nationwide
thereusepeople.org

An Oakland, California–based nonprofit, TRP is devoted to salvaging building materials. It has several retail warehouses fully loaded with everything from roofing materials to doors, windows, and flooring.

URBAN REMAINS
Chicago, IL
urbanremainschicago.com

In a city filled with amazing architectural remnants, Urban Remains sells rescued old wooden millwork (such as newel posts), doors, doorknobs, industrial lighting, and much more. Owner Eric J. Nordstrom also runs BLDG. 51, a museum and archive of "historically important elements from notable Chicago buildings."

BED LINENS

You no longer have to search hard for sheets lacking polyester content. In fact, there are so many standout bedding brands that it's impossible to include them all. But here is a short list of companies that prioritize renewable materials and humane working conditions and wages. In general, when shopping for sheets, duvets, and blankets, look for 100 percent natural materials with OEKO-TEX and GOTS certifications (see page 227). Also check out the mattress brands listed on page 227; most also sell bedding, including hard-to-find items like organic cotton pillow protectors.

AREA
New York, NY, and Los Angeles, CA
areahome.com

Back in 1990, dismayed by the wrinkle-proof, mixed-blend bedsheets dominating the US market, New York–based Swedish designer Anki Spets introduced her natural-fiber bedding. Area continues to specialize in linen and organic cotton sheets and alpaca blankets in muted shades that are all about comfort and casualness (Anki even builds rumples into some of the designs).

BOLL & BRANCH
bollandbranch.com

Podcast listeners may rue the day this start-up launched, its ads so dominated the airwaves for years. Along the way, Boll & Branch has stood by its commitment to treating workers responsibly and to using sustainable raw materials and environmentally conscientious practices. It has grown to be the largest buyer of Fair Trade–Certified organic cotton.

COYUCHI
Point Reyes, CA, and other locations
coyuchi.com

This California company has been spreading the word about organic cotton and linen bedding since 1991. Coyuchi stands out for being scrupulous in its practices, including offering organic sheets in undyed natural shades; see examples on pages 205 and 234.

CULTIVER
cultiver.com

An Australian company that now has a worldwide presence, Cultiver makes soft linen bedding from European flax in a sophisticated, wide-ranging palette.

KOTN
Montreal and Toronto, Canada
kotn.com

A certified B Corp, Kotn sources its staple fiber from the Better Cotton Initiative and 2,390 small-family farms in Egypt, where founder Rami Helali is from. Its sheets are made using only OEKO-TEX–certified nontoxic dyes, and a percentage of proceeds goes to the building of schools in the Nile Delta: to date, Kotn has built seven and funded ten.

MORROW SOFT GOODS
morrowsoftgoods.com

This Los Angeles–based boutique brand takes pride in considered, small-batch production—and in explaining those steps, such as the cold-pad batch-dyeing process. Morrow makes linen and organic cotton sheets, gauze quilts, gingham linen tablecloths, waffle-weave towels, and more.

ROUGH LINEN
roughlinen.com

Inspired by a pillowcase made from flax grown, loomed, and stitched by her great-grandmother in Scotland, Tricia Rose dreamed up her Northern California bedding company. At Remodelista we got to know Tricia as fans of her textured and weighty— but not *actually* rough—European linens (seen on pages 22, 198, and 205). The line is stitched by in-house sewers in Marin County and sold only via the website.

SONOMA WOOL COMPANY
Sonoma, CA
sonomawoolcompany.com

A satisfying alternative to goose down, wool is hypoallergenic and breathable (cooler in summer, warmer in winter). The Sonoma Wool Company sources its wool from family ranches throughout the US and uses it to make a range of things, including wool comforters and mattress toppers. Also worth checking out: Sonoma Wool Company's wool dish-drying mats (see one on page 177), ironing board pads, and wool batting insulation.

TEKLA
teklafabrics.com

In addition to linen and organic cotton bedding and dream duvets, this Danish company makes great unisex sleepwear.

WOOLROOM
thewoolroom.com

UK brand Woolroom sells a range of bedding, including wool-stuffed duvets and mattresses. The company uses only responsibly produced British wool—find their list of farmer suppliers on their website.

BULK SHOPS

When stocking up on food and household staples, avoiding wasteful packaging is tricky, until you discover the world of refill shopping: bring your own bag and containers for everything from flour, grains, pasta, and olive oil to shampoo and laundry detergent. Someday there will likely be many more grocery chains like Unverpackt, Germany's influential package-free store. In the meantime, mom-and-pop bulk shops like Linh Truong's Soap Dispensary in Toronto are turning up all over (see Linh's sustainable beauty tips on page 211). There are also bulk sellers at farmers' markets, bulk shopping sections in supermarkets, and online bulk suppliers. Pinpoint the options near you by consulting the bulk-finder maps at zerowaste.com, zero-waste-movement originator Bea Johnson's website, and litterless.com, a state-by-state resource guide.

FURNITURE

Some of these workshops belong to solo woodworkers, others are sizable businesses; all focus on using responsibly forested wood and sustainable materials to make heirloom-quality modern designs.

ANOTHER COUNTRY
London, England
anothercountry.com

British tastemaker Paul de Zwart's craft furniture company produces contemporary versions of archetypal British country furniture, such as the oak table for two on page 232. A carbon-neutral business with a showroom in London's Marylebone neighborhood, Another Country uses only natural materials, and follows best manufacturing practices, including planting more trees than it uses and providing a repair-and-restore service.

BLACK CREEK MERCANTILE & TRADING CO.
Kingston, NY
blackcreekmt.com

A small, influential workshop led by furniture maker and wooden spoon maestro Joshua Vogel, Black Creek Mercantile specializes in trestle tables, serving boards with carved handles, and other pared-back classic forms. Signature finish: blackened oak.

BRIAN PERSICO
Windham, NY
brianpersico.com

Furniture maker Brian Persico is a locavore and a purist: he uses wood sourced within 20 miles (32 kilometers) of his Catskills studio and mixes his own glues and finishes using centuries-old recipes. His family compound, as seen on pages 29–45, showcases his work, which is rooted in American farmhouse staples—"pieces that were used every day, often as a means for survival," he says—from step stools to stair railings. Brian has a web shop and also makes pieces for BDDW's showrooms, FAIR in New York, and MARCH in San Francisco.

CISCO HOME
Culver City and Pasadena, CA, plus retailers across the country
cisco.com

For thirty-plus years, this California company has been synonymous with green-minded, comfy sofas and other upholstered pieces, including a Victorian-inspired collection by John Derian. On the Cisco materials menu: FSC-certified woods, organic latex, jute, hemp, wool, and organic cotton. Pieces are made to order by hand in South Central Los Angeles, where Cisco runs community woodworking and other mentoring programs.

DeVOL
Cotes Mill and London, England, and New York, NY
devolkitchens.com

In addition to its standout line of kitchen designs, deVOL offers some choice furnishings, such as a wall-hung vegetable bin, a wooden plate rack, and the bestselling Bum Stool, "designed to be the comfiest stool you'll ever sit on." That's deVOL's cedar Clothes Horse laundry rack on our back cover.

EMECO
Hanover, PA
emeco.net

Emeco was founded in 1944 to produce "lightweight, noncorrosive, fire-resistant, and torpedo-proof" chairs for the US Navy. Made from scrap aluminum and still in production, the original Navy chair is a model of utility and good design. Now working with big-name designers (Jasper Morrison, Frank Gehry, Philippe Starck). Emeco continues to produce innovative seating from recycled materials, such as PET, cork, and green concrete.

KALON STUDIOS
kalonstudios.com

"We always approach the pieces with a timeless intent and longevity," says Michaele Simmering, who runs the Los Angeles studio with her husband, Johannes Pauwen. The two have fine-tuned a Southern California take on minimalist, Scandinavian-style furnishings, all made in the US from wood local to their factory.

SAWKILLE CO.
Rhinebeck, NY
sawkille.com

Hands-on makers of what's been termed "rural American design," artist-craftsman Jonah Meyer and creative director Tara DeLisio run a no-waste production shop and a showroom in New York's Hudson Valley. "A deep appreciation and study of the historic has allowed us to develop our distinct furniture expression," writes Tara.

SEBASTIAN COX
London, England
sebastiancox.co.uk

With his own zero-waste, carbon-conscious workshop, studio, and showroom, Sebastian Cox is a leader of the UK's "conscious design" movement. In addition to designing a wide range of wooden furniture, including standout rift-sawn oak kitchen cabinets for deVOL, he experiments with new materials: his hanging lights have compostable shades made from mycelium and wood waste. To measure environmental impact, every piece is given a life cycle assessment. As a sideline business, Sebastian runs a portable mill specializing in "planking" felled trees otherwise destined for the wood chipper.

SKAGERAK
Copenhagen, Denmark, and retailers worldwide
skagerak.dk

Established in 1976, Skagerak is a family-owned business—and Certified B Corp (see page 226)—devoted to designing simple, functional Danish modern furniture for indoors and out. The company has been using FSC-certified wood since 2003, and resells used pieces as Skagerak Reclassics (see page 326). Its oak drying rack (seen on page 176) is shipped in cardboard entirely free of any other materials.

GENERAL HOUSEHOLD GOODS: US EDITION

These emporiums supply inspired versions of everyday necessities.

BOSTON GENERAL STORE
Brookline and Dedham, MA
bostongeneralstore.com

Purveyors of plastic-free, reusable goods, from French net market bags to glass salt pots.

BROOK FARM GENERAL STORE
brookfarmgeneralstore.com

Brook Farm offers a far-ranging collection of useful objects gathered the world over, including Finnish merino wool blankets, wooden scrub brushes from Germany, and Moroccan market baskets.

CANOE
Portland, OR
canoe.design

This indie gallery sells timeless designs, like the canoe that "performs its function splendidly." The company's offerings are eye-opening: from Korbo's Swedish wire fishermen's baskets to the L. Ercolani classic Utility Stacking Chair.

FLOTSAM + FORK
flotsamandfork.com

Flotsam + Fork stocks old-fashioned European—especially French—kitchenware, such as ceramic utensil jars, bistro dish towels, and wicker laundry baskets (see page 197).

GENERAL STORE
San Francisco and Venice, CA
shop-generalstore.com

A hipster home goods store with a California vibe. Get your Wonder Valley olive oil, Fat and the Moon potions, and Humble Ceramics coffee drippers here.

HELEN MILAN
helenmilan.com

Helen Milan is a New England–based online shop that spotlights well-designed wares from indie businesses, including several of the items pictured on page 187.

SALTER HOUSE
Brooklyn Heights, NY
salter.house

Shopkeeper-curator Sandeep Salter's artful emporium and tea room is a Remodelista haunt: you can stop for a pastry and a natural dish scrubber—then pop next door to Sandeep's print gallery, Picture Room.

SUGAR TOOLS
Camden, ME
sugartoolsshop.com

Amy O'Donnell worked in the New York design world before moving to midcoast Maine and setting up shop on Camden's aptly named Bay View Street. Sugar Tools is open seasonally, from May through December, but its goods are sold online year-round. It's the place to find exemplary versions of made-in-Maine classics, such as onion baskets, balsam pillows, and woven wastebaskets, as well as iron coat hooks, mushroom knives, and other finds from farther afield.

SUNNY'S POP
Narrowsburg, NY
sunnyspop.com

Several years ago, Sunrise Coigney opened a pop-up shop in Callicoon, New York, near where she and her husband, actor and environmental activist Mark Ruffalo, have a house. Sunny's Pop was so popular that it found a permanent home on Main Street in the village of Narrowsburg. An actress with an eye for design, Sunny specializes in objects she describes as "sustainably manufactured as well as timeless," like antique Eastlake slipper chairs, recycled-wool tartan blankets, and Japanese *donabe*.

TORTOISE GENERAL STORE
Venice, CA
tortoisegeneralstore.com

Tortoise is Venice Boulevard's hub of "slow and steady" design from Japan. Hasami Porcelain, owner Taku Shinomoto's line of stackable ceramic tableware, is displayed in its own showroom within the store.

THE VERMONT COUNTRY STORE
Weston and Rockingham, VT
www.vermontcountrystore.com

Established in 1946, Vrest and Mildred Ellen Orton's Vermont Country Store was intended as a community gathering place and source for "the practical and hard-to-find." It's still owned and run by the Orton family—seventh- and eighth-generation Vermonters and fourth- and fifth-generation storekeepers. And true to the founding motto, its two stores and unabashedly dowdy catalog are filled with things you don't often see, such as egg poacher pans, metal jar openers, and all-wool dust mops.

GENERAL HOUSEHOLD GOODS: GLOBAL EDITION

Run by visionary shopkeepers, the spots on this list are akin to museums of the inspired object. All sell online and most also have brick-and-mortar locations that we make a beeline for when in Madrid—or Mexico City or Marseille.

A.G. HENDY & CO HOME STORE
Hastings, England
aghendy.com/shop

"I am not an ornament person," says chef and photographer Alastair Hendy. "I like practical things, such as scissors, brushes, and string." He sells top-drawer versions of these in the most magical of settings: a restored three-story town house in Hastings's Old Town that looks like an early Victorian dry goods store. Home Store Kitchen, Alastair's seafood restaurant, is in the back.

BAILEYS
Ross-on-Wye, England
baileyshome.com

Expert stylists Mark and Sally Bailey are the UK's long-reigning king and queen of upcycling. At their farm emporium in Herefordshire and in their many books—such as *Recycled Home*, *Imperfect Home*, and *Handmade Home*—they showcase patinated objects given new uses. "Forget preconceived ideas about the purpose of things," they write. In their store, that translates as jeans recycled as rag rugs, garden trugs made from used tires, and a full line of weathered wood benches, stools, and chairs.

BERDOULAT
Bath, England
berdoulat.co.uk

Patrick and Neri Williams's design studio specializes in stylish historic restoration in Bath, England, the epicenter of Georgian architecture. Having spent years collaborating with area artisans on antique-inspired housewares and furniture—wooden egg racks, willow bread baskets, spice dressers—the couple recently opened a shop in a revived 1768 storefront.

CASA GONZÁLEZ & GONZÁLEZ
Madrid, Spain
gonzalez-gonzalez.es

This tiny spot in Madrid's Salesas district is the creation of childhood friends with a passion for timeless, utilitarian wares, and a knack for design themselves. The emphasis is on goods made by family-owned manufacturers who use natural materials. Some standouts: German oak doorstops, tins of Portuguese wood wax, and Casa González & González's own copper-and-brass trays and candleholders.

ELLEI HOME
Edinburgh, Scotland
elleihome.com

A collection of soulful, handmade goods from the UK and beyond (of special note: Kirsten Hecktermann's cushions in hand-dyed velvet). Owner Nina Plummer writes on the website about "considered homemaking." Originally online only and called Ingredients LDN, the business changed names in 2021 and opened a test lab/showroom in Edinburgh's historic New Town.

EVERYDAY NEEDS
Auckland, New Zealand
everyday-needs.com

A compendium of household details, Everyday Needs sells "the pared back, earthy, and honest." The site is a Remodelista favorite for armchair browsing.

FATHER RABBIT
Auckland, New Zealand
fatherrabbit.com

Claudia Zinzan began by selling simple, traditional housewares—wood-handled dusters, brass hooks—from a "rabbit-sized" corner of her own home. Her selections and displays were such a success that Claudia and her husband, Nick, now run five retail locations in Auckland, showcasing well-made accessories for every room.

GOODEE
goodeeworld.com

Twins Byron and Dexter Peart's B Corp–certified marketplace is devoted to promoting thoughtful consumerism: sourced from around the world, its "purposeful home goods" are made of natural or upcycled materials and come with stories of ethically treated artisans, heritage craft preservation, water conservancy, and community engagement. For an example of what they sell, take a look at the kapok-stuffed bedrolls on page 108, and read the Pearts' tips on how to be a better shopper on page 239.

JUNE
Winnipeg, MB, Canada
junehomesupply.com

Proprietors Danielle and Joël Cyr specialize in mood-elevating details, such as fragrant lavender water for spritzing on linens. Their quiet photos of rope doormats and wicker laundry hampers are odes to the everyday.

LABOUR AND WAIT
London, England (four locations), and Tokyo, Japan
labourandwait.co.uk

At Remodelista, we've always had a thing for beautiful household tools: enamelware dustpans, galvanized metal buckets, and other pre-plastic stalwarts. And for a very long time, Labour and Wait was one of the world's sole suppliers of such things. It's now far from alone, but remains the standard-bearer.

MAISON EMPEREUR
Marseille, France
empereur.fr

All the essentials once offered by France's now shuttered traditional neighborhood kitchen emporiums can still be found at Maison Empereur—along with hardware items, bathroom goods, toys, and a slew of classic French staples for the home, from wicker chairs to enameled sinks. Opened in 1827, this family-run institution has the distinction of being the oldest hardware and cookware shop in the country.

MANUFACTUM
Waltrop and twelve other locations in Germany; Vienna, Austria
manufactum.com

Find more than two thousand well-manufactured, hard-wearing goods, from slatted beechwood produce bins to steel trash cans, at this German department store. The business was founded in 1988 by Thomas Hoof, former managing director of the German Green Party in North Rhine–Westphalia.

MERCI
Paris, France
merci-merci.com

Reason enough to make a trip to Paris: Merci's charmingly French collection of home furnishings and desk and garden supplies. First stop: the linens department, to take in the impossible-to-find-anywhere-else colors. A portion of Merci's proceeds go to education projects in Madagascar and an agro-ecological farm in the Île-de-France.

OBJECTS OF USE
Oxford, England
objectsofuse.com

The owner of this Oxford establishment describes it as "a modern day hardware store of household tools made with practiced skill, using low-impact methods and materials." That includes Welsh tapestry blankets, Japanese knives, and brooms and brushes in all shapes and sizes.

UTILITARIO MEXICANO
Mexico City, Mexico
utilitariomexicano.com

When designers Enrique Arellano and Libia Moreno moved to Mexico City from Colombia, they fell in love with the enamelware mugs, stovetop sandwich toasters, and cast-iron pans at the city's markets. Utilitario Mexicano is an ode to their adopted country and its local industries, many in danger of extinction. The goods, all made in Mexico, are artfully arrayed and also available via a robust web shop.

UTILITY
Brighton, England
utilitygreatbritain.co.uk

In a corner store in the seaside town of Brighton, Martha Tiffin holds court amid a collection of "no-nonsense household goods." "We sell things that are designed so well that there's been no need to change their format in many years or ever," she says. When Tiffin couldn't find a toilet brush and holder up to her standards, she designed her own (see the photo on page 213).

ZANGRA
zangra.com

While renovating an 1850 hotel, Belgian architect Eve Van Dyck and designer Thierry Donnay were inspired by its porcelain sconces and switches—and soon found themselves in the business of reintroducing classic lighting designs that had been out of production. In addition to Zangra-made designs, they sell staples for the home made by small European factories, such as rattan carpet beaters, porcelain window handles, and wall-hung knobs of soap (like the one on page 67).

MATTRESSES

To prioritize green options, look for natural materials—latex made from the sap of rubber trees, hemp or organic cotton, wool, recycled steel coils—as well as rigorous third-party certifications, such as GOLS (the Global Organic Latex Standard; see "Look for These Labels" on page 227 and "Build a Better Bed" on page 200). It's also essential to ensure that chemical flame retardants have not been applied. Within those parameters, it's a crowded, hype-filled market, but there are a lot of good options; we've included but a sampling.

AVOCADO
Santa Monica, CA, and eight other US cities
avocadogreenmattress.com

Made of organic latex, wool, and cotton with pocketed springs—a design known as a latex hybrid—the Avocado Green Mattress is one of only three mattresses certified by MADE SAFE, which screens against 6,500 chemicals related to human and planetary health (Naturepedic and Happsy are the other two). Avocado manufactures its mattresses in its own California factory. It also makes organic linen and cotton bedding and bed pillows filled with kapok.

AWARA
awarasleep.com

Awara ships its latex-hybrid mattresses directly and offers a 365-night trial. Its latex is Rainforest Alliance certified, but the mattresses themselves, which are manufactured in China, are not certified organic. For each mattress sold, Awara donates funds to nonprofit Trees for the Future for the planting of ten fruit trees.

BIRCH BY HELIX
birchliving.com

Birch is bed-in-a-box brand Helix's answer to the organic mattress movement. Materials used: New Zealand wool, natural Talalay latex certified by the eco-INSTITUT of Germany, GOTS organic cotton, and American steel. The mattresses are American made and shipped via FedEx.

COCO-MAT
Locations worldwide
coco-mat.com

A Greek company that's now global, Coco-Mat has been in the business of making natural-materials mattresses since 1989. "Coco" in the name refers to the coconut fibers that are combined with natural latex to make "elasticized coconut fiber." You can test its mattresses at hotels around the world (see the locator on its website) and at Coco-Mat stores—there are three in New York City alone.

HAPPSY
happsy.com

Certified organic in its entirety, the Happsy mattress (which comes compressed in a box) is made in the US from layers of wool batting, latex, organic cotton fabric and filling, and pocketed springs made from recycled metal. Nice feature: It has a zipper for easy access to the internal components, making recycling easier.

MY GREEN MATTRESS
mygreenmattress.com

A family-owned company that operates its own GOTS- and GOLS-certified factory in La Grange Highlands, Illinois, My Green Mattress focuses on offering better lumbar support, more latex padding, and more organic wool (as a quilted top layer) than the competition.

NATUREPEDIC
Locations across the US and Canada
naturepedic.com

Launched by an environmental engineer to provide chemical-free crib mattresses, Naturepedic largely employs Amish craftspeople in its factory outside Cleveland. The company is perhaps the most scrupulous of mattress businesses, and its line has received the full slate of certifications and endorsements.

PARACHUTE
Venice, CA, and eleven other US locations
parachutehome.com

Best known for its OEKO-TEX–certified cotton bedding, Parachute makes a single mattress, medium hard, composed of New Zealand wool, organic cotton, and tempered steel coils (no natural latex, which, the company points out, deteriorates over time).

PLUSHBEDS
plushbeds.com

PlushBeds fabricates its range of Greenguard-, GOLS- and GOTS-, and USDA Organic–certified mattresses north of Los Angeles. It also makes bedding, including wool mattress toppers and wool pillows.

SPINDLE
spindlemattress.com

The Spindle classic is made in the US by fourth-generation mattress makers and sold via their website. Interesting wrinkle: Customers assemble the latex layers at home, a two-person job that enables the level of firmness to be adjusted. The company also sells layers of latex, should you want to refresh your bed.

PAINT AND PLASTER

Zero- or low-VOC paints are easy to find these days. But the paint most brands sell is latex, which is made of acrylic resins, a liquid plastic. (See more on the subject on page 230.) A better option: age-old natural finishes such as limewash and milk paint. They're currently specialized and pricey—and not always as easy to apply as latex—but we predict they'll be coming soon to a paint store near you.

AFM SAFECOAT
afmsafecoat.com

A forty-year-old business focused on developing building and cleaning products for people with chemical sensitivities, Safecoat began by making a sealant for use in hospitals. It offers stains and finishes as well as plant- and mineral-based paints and primers, all formulated in consultation with doctors for "the least possible toxicity."

AMERICAN CLAY
americanclay.com

Popular in the UK and making inroads in the US, matte-textured clay plaster has moisture-absorbing (and desorbing) abilities that make it a humidity regulator. It comes in powdered form that gets mixed with water and tinted with clay pigments made from oxides and ochers (the company explains of its palette: "If you have seen it in nature, you can find it here"). Clay plaster can be applied over drywall and many other surfaces, including wallpaper, but splash zones in baths and kitchens need to be sealed.

ANNIE SLOAN
anniesloan.com

Decorative painter Annie Sloan introduced her well-known line of chalk paints in 1990 for use on furniture, cabinets, walls, and floors. It can also be applied over brick and stone, and no primer is needed on most surfaces. The paint can be left as is, with its chalky, matte finish, or, if used in an area subject to wear and tear, sealed with a protective layer of wax.

BAUWERK COLOUR
bauwerkcolour.com

Bauwerk produces lime paint, a finish concocted from a mix of clay, minerals, and natural pigments (a thinner version composed of lime putty is known as limewash). It's best applied to masonry, such as brickwork, and also plaster; surfaces that have already been painted require a special primer. Lime paint has a distinctive luminosity and a depth of color—see a Bauwerk white on the brick stair on page 118.

BEECK MINERAL PAINTS
beeckmineralpaints.com

A North Carolina company originally founded in Germany in 1894, Beeck specializes in mineral silicate paints for stucco, concrete, brick, and other masonry surfaces. Rather than forming a surface film, silicate paint bonds with its substrate—as do limewash and clay paints—and is widely used on the exteriors and interiors of historic structures.

BIOSHIELD PAINT COMPANY
bioshieldpaint.com

BioShield's clay paint comes ready mixed and is composed of natural clays and mineral pigments. The company makes other solvent-free, zero-VOC surface coatings, including wood stains, oils, waxes, and soaps.

CLAYWORKS
clay-works.com

The clay-based plaster finishes of this UK maker have been put to use by some of our favorite architects everywhere from cabins to lofts; peruse the Clayworks site's "Case Studies" for inspiration.

COLOUR MAKES PEOPLE HAPPY
East Sussex, England
colourmakespeoplehappy.com

Simon March runs the ultimate neighborhood paint shop, with jarred pigments lining the walls and a paint bar where colors are mixed by hand and given names like "Genial Outrage." Simon's blends use local ingredients from the South Downs, including lime putty, linseed oil, chalk, and alabaster, and he hangs painted Dutch wooden shoes to show sample shades. His advice on how to choose a color? "You'll get more inspiration from a vegetable stall than a swatch book."

DOMINGUE ARCHITECTURAL FINISHES
Houston, TX
dominguefinishes.com

This offshoot of Houston's Chateau Domingue, vendor of grand European antiques, sells finishes ideal for the settings its pieces land in. Curated by artisan painter Eddy Dankers (client roster: the royal family of Belgium and designer Axel Vervoordt), the collection includes plasters, limewash, and mineral paints heretofore hard to find in the US.

EARTH+FLAX
earthandflax.com

Natalie Yon-Eriksson's Philadelphia business imports Scandinavian linseed oil products for restoring, painting, and cleaning wood. Customers can schedule a consult by phone to learn about uses for Earth+Flax's lines, which include falun, the iron-oxide pigmented finish used in Sweden to paint houses red.

ECOS PAINTS
Spartanburg, SC
ecospaints.net

This US company has supplied its latex-free paints to the Louvre, Westminster Abbey, and the Getty. ECOS manufactures all its products in South Carolina, including a line of specialty finishes for people with chemical sensitivities, asthma, and allergies. Its ingredients, which are detailed on its site for every product, fulfill the requirements of the Declare label and are Red List Free (see page 226 for more on these designations).

EDWARD BULMER NATURAL PAINT
edwardbulmerpaint.co.uk

Interior designer Edward Bulmer collaborates with German paint company AURO to make "paint that does not cost the earth." Key ingredients: plant-based binders, linseed oil, and what the company describes as "the twelve natural earth and mineral pigments that have been used by artists for centuries." Every step of the production process is carbon neutral, and nothing is produced that can't be composted or recycled.

GRAPHENSTONE
graphenstoneusa.com

An innovative line run by a chemical engineer in Seville, Spain, Graphenstone makes lime paint reinforced with graphene, a recently engineered material known for being thin, strong, durable, and highly conductive. The Cradle to Cradle Gold–certified paint (see page 226) is being developed to improve the thermal regulation of buildings, meaning it could make structures require less heating and air-conditioning.

GREEN PLANET PAINTS
greenplanetpaints.com

Green Planet Paints is a small Arizona-based collection of architectural paints, stains, sealers and colorants made from mineral clays and plant oils. We used their AgriPaint in our "Furniture Makeover with Paint" on page 289.

KALKLITIR
kalklitir.com

Kalklitir's limewash comes in powdered formulas that when mixed with water can be brushed on just about any primed surface. Remodelista editor Justine Hand and her husband, Chad, limewashed their bedroom with Kalklitir's Palladio and Ivory (see the photo on page 198). Find helpful how-to-apply limewash short videos on the Kalklitir site.

LIMESTRONG
limestrongartisan.com

When self-described "lifelong plasterer and lime geek" Ryan Chivers couldn't find an easy-to-apply lime plaster made with US-sourced ingredients, he concocted his own. His signature product, Limestrong, is a mineral finish composed of Ohio lime, Idaho pumice, and "a small quantity of a plant-based binder," colored with eight mineral pigments. Olive oil soap can be used to seal the finish. Ryan also sells limewash, tadelakt (polished, water-resistant Moroccan plaster), and sample kits for experimenting.

MASTER OF PLASTER
masterofplaster.com

Master of Plaster are architectural preservationists—you can see their work on the ceilings of New York's Grand Central Terminal—and purveyors of slaked lime plasters (composed of limestone that's been baked at high temperatures to remove impurities and hydrated). It comes in an aged putty form, so unlike other options, you don't have to hand mix it—but like all plasters, troweling it takes skill (and several coats). Resident designer Lauren Dillon is a fount of information on how to use their products, which, she points out, once cured "look and feel like stone."

PORTOLA PAINTS & GLAZES
North Hollywood, CA
portolapaints.com

A Los Angeles go-to for specialty wall finishes, Portola mixes its own limewash and Roman clay in small batches. It's owned by brothers Jamie and Casey Davis, who offer a color-matching service by eye rather than computer.

PURE & ORIGINAL
pure-original.com

This Dutch line of chalk and lime paints and plaster decorative finishes is made in a small family-owned paint factory in Belgium. See Pure & Original lime paint on the walls of the Rescued Relic on page 128.

REAL MILK PAINT CO.
realmilkpaint.com

American colonists mixed their interior house paint from a combination of curdled milk, lime, pigments, and water. The milk protein casein is the key ingredient in milk paint, which has a distinct chalky look and feel (it's akin to chalk paint but thinner). Milk paint can be applied to furniture and walls, no primer needed, but be warned that it wears and chips easily. Real Milk Paint Co.'s paints get mixed with water just before being applied and remain usable for two weeks after.

ROMABIO
romabio.com

Romabio makes mineral-based products, including exterior limewash that's sold at Home Depot and other retailers. The Athens, Georgia, company's interior mineral paints come in four finishes: low luster, super flat, matte, and satin.

UNEARTHED PAINTS
unearthedpaints.com

Composed of raw ingredients like clay, chalk, marble, and natural pigments, Unearthed Paints (and plasters and wood finishes) are made by Kreidezeit Naturfarben of Germany. They're biodegradable and most are vegan (rather than relying on casein, the protein in their mix comes from plants). Shades range from spinel yellow to umber green and iron-oxide black.

RUGS

Aside from choosing a rug made of natural, replenishable fibers, such as wool and sisal, you should also "interrogate the backing," advises Jonsara Ruth of the Parsons School of Design Healthy Materials Lab. "Carpets can have five or six layers, which is what you don't want. A simple jute weave is ideal." And be sure to look out for the right third-party certifications (see page 226). The best option for the environment, of course, is going with a vintage or antique rug, preferably purchased locally.

ARMADILLO
usa.armadillo-co.com

In 2021, Armadillo became the first Australian rug brand to earn B Corporation certification, and its full product line carries the Declare label (see page 226). The company donates 10 percent of its net profits, via its foundation, to bettering education in underserved communities.

ARONSON'S
New York, NY
aronsonsfloors.com

With its large collection of wall-to-wall carpeting as well as finished area rugs from a who's who of reputable brands, many from Europe, this family business is a go-to resource for New York City designers. It's helmed by architect Carol Swedlow, daughter of the company's founders, who has made environmental sustainability one of its core tenets.

AUDA SINDA
audasinda.com

Every rug from this artisan studio in Bellingham, Washington, is handwoven to order using domestically sourced materials. Its Melange line is made from leftover yarn, and as of 2021, Auda Sinda has doubled down on its sustainability goals, reducing, for instance, its reliance on latex (which is natural but comes in plastic jugs) in the finishing process.

BOLÉ ROAD TEXTILES
boleroadtextiles.com

A few years ago, when we first stumbled upon Ethiopian-born Hana Getachew's textiles business, she was offering just pillows, throws, and bath mats via her website and Brooklyn studio. Today, Bolé Road has expanded to include table linens, curtains, accessories, and Ethiopian wool rugs, all woven by artisans in her homeland. (And the brand is now also available at West Elm and Design Within Reach.) Its colorful rugs are made in a Fair Trade–certified facility.

HOOK AND LOOM
hookandloom.com

Rugs from this Berkshires company come in only three natural materials: 100 percent recycled cotton, undyed wool, or organic cotton. In addition, no dyes, chemicals, or latex are used to create its products. (That's their loom-hooked wool design on page 200.)

MAHARAM
maharam.com

A long-standing New York company selling textiles by Ray and Charles Eames and other '60s greats, Maharam is now owned by Herman Miller and has showrooms all over the world. Its collection of rugs includes designs by Alexander Girard and Hella Jongerius (see an example on page 236). We admire Maharam's anti-greenwashing stance, detailed on their website's "Environmental Position" page: every product description includes a section on its environmental credentials.

MERIDA RUGS
meridastudio.com

This exemplary Fall River, Massachusetts, workshop gets its wool from New Zealand and UK sources that adhere to strict animal treatment regulations. It avoids synthetic and oil-based fibers in all stages of the manufacturing process, and donates scrap yarns to the textile programs at the nearby Rhode Island School of Design and UMass Dartmouth.

MINNA
minna-goods.com

Founded by Sara Berks in 2013, Minna specializes in textiles—including cotton and wool modern rugs—handwoven by artisans in Mexico and South America. The B Corp company strives for transparency and ethical practices in the manufacturing process.

NORDIC KNOTS
nordicknots.com

A good resource for Scandinavian rugs, Nordic Knots's pieces are designed in Stockholm and handmade using New Zealand wool by craftspeople in Bhadohi, India, and are GoodWeave certified.

PRÏVATE0204
Copenhagen, Denmark
Private0204shop.com

The Danish rug company specializes in vintage hemp rugs that have been restored, repaired (often via visible patches), "washed in the sea, and dried on the beach." See one in situ on page 22.

REVIVAL
revivalrugs.com

A direct-to-consumer disruptor, Revival carries its own line of natural, azo-free dyed rugs, but it's perhaps best known for its collection of vintage Turkish rugs, all of which get tumbled, washed, and groomed. Then, depending on condition and style, each is either overdyed, antique-washed, or left as is. For the most eco-friendly options, peruse its Original Vintage and Kilim lines.

SHARKTOOTH
Brooklyn, NY
sharktoothnyc.com

We've long admired the textiles store founded by photographer Kellen Tucker for its selection of vintage blankets and rugs, which are sourced entirely from estate sales, auctions, and flea markets. They include Amish rag rugs, antique Chinese floor coverings, Turkish kilims, South American flat weaves, and more. Each is cleaned and restored before listing.

SHIPROCK SANTA FE
Santa Fe, NM
shiprocksantafe.com

This gallery was founded by fifth-generation art dealer Jed Foutz, who grew up on a Navajo reservation in New Mexico. It specializes in Native American artwork, ceramics, jewelry, and furniture, but it's Shiprock's rug room that has made it Instagram-famous. In it, you'll find a vast assortment of hand-spun and -woven Navajo designs, some dating back to the 1800s.

TANTUVI
tantuvistudio.com

The Brooklyn-based rug company was started by Arati Rao to spotlight the artistry of Indian textile weavers. Tantuvi works with a community of twenty-six families who bring Rao's bold, abstract designs to life. Its hemp, cotton, and silk rugs are hand-dyed in small batches using nontoxic dyes.

WILLABY
willabyshop.com

This Georgia-based design studio specializes in organic cotton children's bedding and accessories, but it also happens to carry great-looking basic cotton rugs for anywhere in the house. Hand-loomed by Amish weavers using absolutely no electricity, they're GOTS certified (see page 227) and washable, to boot.

WOODARD & GREENSTEIN
woodardweave.com

From long-standing antiques dealers Blanche Greenstein and Thos. K. Woodward, this line of classic American flat-weave rugs in stripes and checks work especially well as hall runners and area rugs (see a fringed example on page 143). Each is hand-loomed of organic cotton tinted with eco-friendly dyes.

WOODNOTES
woodnotes.fi

The Finnish brand makes good-looking wool rugs, but it's their floor coverings woven from paper yarn that most intrigue us. The traditional Scandinavian material (a twine-like spun paper) is durable, recyclable, and sustainable, and the manufacturing process is powered by green energy.

What to Do with Unwanted Things

A Guide to Responsibly Donating, Selling, Recycling, and More

In the conservation movement, an oft-cited quote is Greenpeace USA executive director Annie Leonard's observation that when things get thrown away, "there is no such thing as 'away.'" What we toss ends up in landfills and oceans, even on mountaintops (plastic filaments have been found in the snow near the summit of Mount Everest, the earth's tallest peak). Curtail this scourge by avoiding disposables, giving away or selling useful goods to keep them in circulation, and sending recyclable materials to the right places. Here's a guide to making that happen.

GIVE AND GET FREE GOODS

From an environmental and social standpoint, sharing resources in your own locale is an ideal option. Thanks to social media, it's easy to post snapshots of what you've got and find eager takers within walking distance. These sites are also a good place to find things you're looking for. Need moving boxes and packing materials, children's gear, basic bookshelves, or a table and chairs? They're all giveaway staples.

Books

LITTLE FREE LIBRARY
littlefreelibrary.org

You've no doubt come across these: there are more than one hundred thousand book-sharing spots in wooden boxes worldwide—on sidewalks, in train stations, near park benches. Use the site's finder map to locate Little Free Libraries near you and drop off some books: the boxes aren't much bigger than birdhouses, so if you have a lot of books to give, you'll have to visit more than one.

Clothes

REHASH CLOTHES
rehashclothes.com

On this nationwide exchange, members list garments up for grabs and receive credits that can be applied to items on the site, all at no cost.

General Goods

BUY NOTHING
buynothingproject.org

Founded in 2013 by two friends on Bainbridge Island, Washington, as "an experimental hyper-local gift economy," Buy Nothing has become a worldwide movement that enables participants to "give where you live." It's divided into local chapters that serve as forums for neighbors to post things they don't need or are looking for, and to take things they can use. These clusters operate as Facebook Groups: you can only join in your own locale, and money is never exchanged. The newer Buy Nothing app allows givers and seekers to share beyond their immediate area.

CRAIGSLIST
craigslist.org

Two of the most popular sections of Craigslist are those devoted to freebies and items for sale. Part of the secret to Craigslist's success is that it doesn't charge for these listings, but the burden of showing the wares and arranging for pickup or delivery is on you.

FACEBOOK MARKETPLACE
facebook.com

A popular spot to sell items locally, Facebook Marketplace also does brisk business in giveaways.

THE FREECYCLE NETWORK
freecycle.org

In addition to posting offers for the taking, you can list things you need on this grassroots nonprofit's network devoted to the sharing of free items. Founded in 2003, Freecycle has local reuse groups the world over.

NEXTDOOR
nextdoor.com

A neighborhood network, Nextdoor operates as a local chat room and bulletin board. Join where you live to give away—and sell—goods locally, and to take in the community scuttlebutt.

Plants

BLOSSM
blossm.garden

An app for privately swapping plants and garden items, as well as buying or selling them.

PLANT SWAP
plantswap.org

Organized plant swaps—gatherings for trading potted plants, cuttings, and other greenery—have become a global phenomenon. Check this website to find one taking place near you. Word is also often spread on social media (if you live in a city, search #plantswap plus your locale).

DONATE

Be part of the reuse chain and help nonprofits in the process. If you have a lot of unwanted stuff, donating it is an easy option, and many organizations will make pickups. Send out only items that are clean and in working order, unless the charity specifies otherwise. And be sure to get a receipt for your tax return.

Clothing

In response to fast fashion, there's a growing movement devoted not only to ethically made garments but also to keeping wearables in use and creating new items from castoffs (see an expert mender's advice on page 291). While general-collection nonprofits like Goodwill and the Salvation Army accept clothing, most sell bales of garments and textiles to developing nations, a practice that's become destructive to local economies—and, after getting shipped, a lot of these discards still end up in dump sites. To avoid this, give to a group with a direct need for what you're donating, such as the following.

CAREER GEAR
careergear.org

If you have gently used suits, button-down shirts, and other "business professional" menswear, this nonprofit is a good recipient: it aids veterans, people post-incarceration, first-generation graduating students, and others who are entering the job market.

DRESS FOR SUCCESS
dressforsuccess.org

Another group devoted to assisting people entering the workforce, Dress for Success collects work-appropriate clothing in more than 25 countries and 150 cities.

HELPSY
helpsy.co

"Clothes aren't trash" is the slogan of this for-profit B Corporation devoted to finding uses for unwanted garments and shoes, whether to be resold in thrift stores or turned into rags for stuffing and insulation. Helpsy serves the Northeast US, and in the past year collected and repurposed 24 million pounds (10.8 million kilograms) of clothes.

ONE WARM COAT
onewarmcoat.org

A donation service that partners with a thousand-plus nationwide nonprofits, One Warm Coat redistributes more than half a million coats annually. Donations can be made at local coat drives and at partner groups listed on the OWC website.

PLANET AID
planetaid.org

A nonprofit whose mission is "To protect the environment and support sustainable development in impoverished communities," Planet Aid is identifiable by its thousands of yellow bins for collecting used clothing, shoes, and household goods. Proceeds go toward vocational training, child aid, and more. The organization partners with Give Back Box (see page 328) so donations can be sent from anywhere.

More and more brands have begun accepting their own used items, which they either resell as is, restore, or recycle. In return, most offer a small credit toward your next purchase. Here are seven labels to note.

COYUCHI

coyuchi.com/secondhome

The organic bedding brand provides a prepaid mailing label for its used linens and loungewear, which get cleaned for resale, upcycled into new items, or recycled. All of this is taken care of by the Renewal Workshop, a group dedicated to "finding the right home for unwanted apparel."

EILEEN FISHER

eileenfisher.com/renew

"You bring back your old pieces, we find them another home—or turn them into entirely new designs." Eileen Fisher's long-standing Renew program was created to extend the lifecycle of its clothes. The company pays $5 per piece in "Renew Rewards," which can be applied at Eileen Fisher stores—many have Renew racks—and online, where you can also shop the Resewn Collection of one-of-a-kind pieces.

GOODWELL

goodwell.co

This toothbrush company will take any oral care products, no matter the manufacturer—toothpaste tubes and dental floss packaging included—and recycle them through TerraCycle (see page 331). Wondering whether this is worthwhile? Consider the fact that a billion toothbrushes get tossed in the US every year, and that they don't degrade—according to Greenpeace, every plastic toothbrush ever made still exists.

IKEA

ikea.com

As part of an overall green initiative—and to push back against its reputation for selling disposable goods—IKEA has begun taking back gently used furniture in exchange for store credit at select stores in the US as well as in twenty-six other countries. The goods are sold in IKEA's "As-Is" sections. The company has also committed to using only renewable and recycled materials globally by 2030.

LEGO REPLAY

givebackbox.com/lego

Send in old and excess bricks, "any and all." In the US, Lego's Replay division works with organizations including Teach For America and the Boys & Girls Clubs of Boston to give more children a chance to play. Lego's goal is to manufacture all its bricks from a new, entirely sustainable material by 2030.

PATAGONIA

patagonia.com

A founding member of the Sustainable Apparel Coalition and a model corporate citizen, Patagonia stands by its vow to take responsibility for their product after they sell it to you. The company's "trade it in to get credit" program accepts used Patagonia items by mail or at Patagonia stores; those donations get restored and resold at stores and via the brand's online Worn Wear shop. To further keep clothes in use, Patagonia offers repair guides and has its own repair center.

SKAGERAK

skagerak.com

The Danish furniture company buys back their used wooden pieces to restore and resell as "Reclassics." "In this way, we honor valuable materials, keep them in circulation, and live up to our promise to create furniture that lasts a lifetime."

Construction Materials

Excess paint, wood, tile, drywall, metal sheeting, replaced cupboards—household building projects always lead to unwieldy leftovers. If you don't know someone who could use what you've got, consider posting a listing on local giveaway sites, such as Craigslist. Here are some nationwide resources.

HABITAT FOR HUMANITY RESTORES
habitat.org

With locations all over the US, this leader in materials reuse accepts construction supplies, including kitchen cabinets, doors, windows, flooring, unused lumber, lighting fixtures, fencing, and bricks, at its ReStores. The donations are used in houses the group builds or offered for sale in the ReStores.

ISCRAP APP
iscrapapp.com

This app directs users to local sites for reselling, repurposing, and recycling metal items, from cars to appliances.

THE REUSE PEOPLE (TRP)
thereusepeople.org

What began in 1993 as a construction-material drive to aid flood victims in Tijuana, Mexico, has grown into a "deconstruction" and social services nonprofit with locations in eight states. TRP is devoted to keeping usable building supplies in circulation. Its trained crews specialize in taking down houses and other structures so their components can be reused.

Electronics

How to keep broken and obsolete equipment out of landfills? Here are resources that make it easy to get these goods where they need to go for reuse and recycling. (For more on the latter, see page 331.)

BEST BUY
bestbuy.com

The nation's largest retail recycler of used electronics and appliances, Best Buy collects old laptops, cell phones, and televisions, as well as appliances and air conditioners, and partners with a recycling group to determine if the products can be reused, repurposed, or recycled. Just show up: customers are limited to three donations per day. Best Buy will also come collect larger items for a fee of $29.99.

HUMAN-I-T
human-i-t.org

A nonprofit social enterprise, Human-I-T provides equipment and training for "communities left on the wrong side of the digital divide," while also diverting technology from the scrap heap. The organization accepts a long list of donated equipment. It wipes devices of sensitive data, then refurbishes, updates, and distributes them.

SECURE THE CALL
securethecall.org

This nonprofit collects unwanted cell phones and tablets and distributes them to aid groups and people in need so they can be used to contact emergency services (all cell phones, whether or not they have an active service contract, are required by law to connect a caller with 911). Lately, most donations have gone to isolated patients in hospitals. The group collects donations in barrels located in more than nine hundred grocery stores, libraries, and police stations, as well as via community drives and through the mail.

Furniture and General Household Goods

The majority of cast-off goods, from chairs to yoga mats, televisions to old tools, can—and should—stay in use. These nationwide charities accept just about everything.

DONATIONTOWN
donationtown.org

A nationwide online directory, DonationTown connects people with local charities "that will actually send a truck to your home to pick up your used clothing and other household items." The site partners with hundreds of organizations that take clothing, furniture, toys, shoes, general household items, and more. Is DonationTown a charity? "No," says its FAQ page. "It's simply here as a resource to help people donate to nonprofit charities. Sometimes doing a good deed is reward enough!"

FURNITURE BANK NETWORK (FBN)
furniturebanks.org

FBN is a consortium of charities throughout North America that collects lightly used furniture and passes it on to those in need. The FBN prevents tens of thousands of chairs, tables, and sofas from ending up in landfills annually. Find a furniture bank near you using the website's locator.

GIVE BACK BOX
givebackbox.com

Give Back Box is a nonprofit founded as a way to make donating easy—and to give a second chance to empty cardboard boxes. Working across the US, Canada, and the UK, the group accepts household goods and clothing; the only stipulation is that filled boxes weigh in at less than 70 pounds (38 kilograms) and measure no more than 9 feet (2.7 meters) long. Participants pay a fee of $15 per box for a UPS shipping label and select a charity to receive the donation from a list of more than one hundred organizations—refugee, environmental, children's groups, and more.

GOODWILL INDUSTRIES INTERNATIONAL
goodwill.org

Located all over the US and Canada, as well as in fourteen other countries, Goodwill accepts furniture and sports equipment, as well as home goods and clothing. Revenue from sales funds the organization's employment-placement services, job-training programs, and other community services.

GREENDROP
gogreendrop.com

GreenDrop collects household items from bedding to electronics, tools to musical instruments. GreenDrop collection sites are in formerly abandoned locations, such as gas stations; pickups are also available. Items are sold in 2nd Ave Thrift Superstores, shipped overseas, or recycled—avoid contributing to the latter two groups by donating only desirable goods. GreenDrop also offers a free home clean-out service. All proceeds go to the American Red Cross, Military Order of the Purple Heart, National Federation of the Blind, and the Society of St. Vincent de Paul.

HABITAT FOR HUMANITY
habitat.org

A global nonprofit dedicated to building community housing, Habitat for Humanity has projects in every state in the US and in more than seventy other countries. Its Habitat ReStores (see page 327) accept donations of tools, appliances, and general household goods, which the stores resell or use in Habitat's affordable housing.

HOMELESS SHELTERS DIRECTORY
homelessshelterdirectory.org

Many homeless shelters can use donations of linens, clothing, and general household items. Use this directory to pinpoint shelters in your area, and then call to find out if your items match their needs.

PICKUPMYDONATION
pickupmydonation.com

PickUpMyDonation is for large items that cannot be moved easily. Free and for-a-fee options depend on where you're located and what you're unloading. The company lets you pick your donation site or will provide you with local suggestions.

THE SALVATION ARMY
salvationarmyusa.org

Founded in London's East End in 1865, the international Christian charity accepts donations of clothing, furniture, household goods, exercise equipment, and appliances. These are sold at Salvation Army shops, and the proceeds are used to fund the group's Adult Rehabilitation Centers.

VIETNAM VETERANS OF AMERICA
vvapickup.org and pickupplease.com

This veterans' support organization accepts donations of clothing, shoes, bedding, toys, books, and small appliances. The website has a drop-off locator, or you can call to schedule a pickup. Items go to VVA programs, including housing, and get sold to provide funds.

Kitchens

This organization is devoted to repurposing everything in the most remodeled room in the house.

GREEN DEMOLITIONS
renovationangel.com/green-demolitions

Founded in 2005 in Greenwich, Connecticut, Green Demolitions (and its sister sites, Kitchen Trader and Renovation Angel) will remove your entire kitchen or bath for free when you're ready to renovate, and sell or recycle the takeaway. Note that the group's focus is on keeping high-end designs in circulation.

Even better than responsibly disposing of unwanted things? Not buying them in the first place. Join the sharing economy: borrow items you're unlikely to use often (and that would take up precious storage space in your home). Instead of buying a tile cutter or giant cake pan, do an online search to see if one's available to loan in your area.

LIBRARY OF THINGS

A worldwide sharing movement, Libraries of Things are collections of borrowable goods of many sorts, from wallpaper steamers to ice cream makers, many of them housed at public libraries, as well as community centers and independent nonprofits. Search "Library of Things" (with quotation marks) plus your city to find what's available near you. Also, turn to these centers to donate desirable goods.

MOOCH

moochapp.com

A free app that lets members search for items they would like to borrow and list things they have available to loan. You can search the app by item or by the person who listed it: "moochers" often know one another and have reciprocal deals going with friends. Sporting and camping equipment, baby gear, and tools are especially popular.

STREETBANK

streetbank.com

A UK neighborhood site that's now global, Streetbank began when two neighbors had a good experience sharing a ladder. It's devoted to making it easy to give away unwanted stuff, lend things that often sit unused, and share skills, such as gardening, cooking, and technical know-how. At sign-up, members are encouraged to offer something in one of these categories.

TOOL LIBRARIES

localtools.org

Tool libraries are an excellent resource for those looking to borrow, not buy. Most are not-for-profit and allow patrons to check out tools, equipment, instruction manuals, and other resources using a library card (some charge a minimal annual membership fee and, as in most libraries, there are fines for late returns). You can find indie tool libraries and tool libraries based in traditional libraries: locate the ones closest to you by consulting the Local Tools map or simply doing an online search.

RECYCLE

Old mattresses, unneeded prescription medicine, ink cartridges—a lot of household stuff, and even some houses themselves, can and should be recycled. Begin by looking up local policies, then turn to the resources listed here. For questions, consult earth911.com, a database of information on how and where to recycle all sorts of things.

Appliances

When household machinery reaches the end of its working life, see to it that it gets scrapped appropriately.

EPA
epa.gov/rad/consumers

The EPA's Responsible Appliance Disposal program lists groups and utilities that pick up and recycle large appliances free of charge.

Batteries

Businesses that gather used electronics, such as Staples and Best Buy, also accept batteries for recycling. So does IKEA, in its customer service/returns department. The MOM's Organic Market chain also makes it easy by offering recycling centers—for batteries, corks, cell phones, oyster shells, and more—in its store entryways; we hope more markets follow suit. Search online for "battery recycling near me" to find the nearest location and requirements.

CALL2RECYCLE
call2recycle.org

A battery and cell phone recycling and stewardship program, Call2Recycle has over thirty thousand collection sites throughout the US and Canada at chains such as Home Depot and Lowe's, as well as at hardware stores and hospitals. The group recovers materials from rechargeable and single-use batteries for use as new batteries—and for producing silverware, pots and pans, and golf clubs. Cell phones get refurbished for resale or used for parts.

Carpets and Rugs

The floor coverings that get tossed in Dumpsters are largely nonbiodegradable polyester. Divert your rugs and carpets from the landfill whenever possible.

CARPET AMERICA RECOVERY EFFORT (CARE)
carpetrecovery.org

A nonprofit founded in 2002 by the carpet industry in collaboration with government agencies, CARE doesn't collect carpets but directs individuals and businesses to places they can go to recycle them. Consult the group's Carpet Collector Finder Map.

CARPETCYCLE
carpetcycle.com

This New Jersey outfit provides carpet removal services as well as recycling: using a shearing system, they break down carpeting for reuse as, among other things, yarn for new carpets and insulation. One of CarpetCycle's past projects was removing and recycling more than a million pounds (over 450,000 kilograms) of material from a Manhattan skyscraper.

Clothing and Textiles

Only about 15 percent of discarded textiles, from socks to curtains, get recycled, leaving 11 million tons in US municipal waste each year, according to the EPA. Fortunately, there's a very active movement afoot to keep cloth in use.

BLUE JEANS GO GREEN
bluejeansgogreen.org

Turning denim into cotton-fiber insulation is the mandate of the Blue Jeans Go Green program. Farmers' markets across the country and Boy Scout troops are among the groups that hold denim drives for the nonprofit. Blue jeans, as well as denim shirts, shorts, and jackets, are accepted in any condition; they just need to be 90 percent cotton. The company also works with fashion brands such as Levi Strauss & Co. and Madewell, which take back their own denim items and send them to Blue Jeans Go Green. (See more take-back options on page 326.) The Zappos for Good program provides free prepaid shipping labels. A portion of the resulting insulation is contributed to Habitat for Humanity and other building charities.

GREEN TREE TEXTILES
greentreetextiles.org

A service focused on recycling fabric, Green Tree partners with nonprofits and local farmers' markets to collect clothes, linens, shoes, and accessories. No donations go to waste: they're either sent to charities or to fiber and rag manufacturers. See the website locator for drop-off locations.

RETRIEVR
retrievr.com

A textile and electronic-waste recycling group, Retrievr offers a free collection service. Garments are sorted and about 30 percent get resold. Much of the rest gets turned into new recycled-content cotton and wool garments by the group's fashion partners.

Construction Materials

"Deconstruction rather than demolishment" is the rallying cry of the circular design movement. Instead of tearing down buildings, the idea is to mine salvageable parts. It's more work, yes, but less wasteful—some cities, such as Portland, Oregon, and Palo Alto, California, have ordinances that require older houses to be taken apart. The same companies that accept construction donations participate in recycling programs; find more of these on page 327, and see our list of architectural salvage dealers on page 312.

CONSTRUCTION & DEMOLITION RECYCLING ASSOCIATION (CDRA)
cdrecycling.org

An umbrella group of construction recycling businesses, the CDRA website has a "find a recycler" section that directs users to local places that accept everything from land-clearing debris to asphalt, roofing shingles, wood waste, and concrete.

Electronics

There ought to be a next life for your laptop or cell phone or their parts. See page 327 for companies that accept electronics donations for repurposing as well as recycling.

EPA
epa.gov/recycle

The EPA's recycling site will point you to electronic waste certification programs, through which you can find an accredited electronics recycler.

NATIONAL CENTER FOR ELECTRONICS RECYCLING (NCER)
electronicsrecycling.org

NCER is a 501(c)(3) dedicated to "the development and enhancement of a national infrastructure for the recycling of used electronics in the US." Find information on its site about why and how to recycle, and follow the link to Greener Gadgets' excellent recycle locator.

STAPLES
staples.com

In partnership with Electronic Recyclers International, Staples accepts old electronics: just drop off donations at any customer service desk (limited to seven items per customer per day). They will even pay you for some used electronics. Staples also works with the records and information services company Iron Mountain to offer a free, environmentally responsible shredding service.

Hard-to-Recycle Items

A lot of everyday trash has no good place to go. The companies listed here are helping to broaden what's recyclable. If you wonder how so many "zero-wasters" manage to accumulate only a single mason jar of trash every year, these companies are part of the answer.

HOW2RECYCLE
how2recycle.info

A division of the environmental nonprofit BlueGreen Alliance, How2Recycle makes it possible to recycle a lot of flexible plastic packaging. In How2Recycle bins at retailers such as Walmart, Staples, Target, and Whole Foods, you can return plastic bags, plastic film, plastic wraps (the kind that comes around packs of things), plastic mail pouches, even broken-down Bubble Wrap, which get turned into synthetic lumber for use as outdoor decking and benches, among other things. The group is also focused on standardizing recycling labels to create a clear way to reuse goods.

TERRACYCLE
terracycle.com

Search "recycle anything," and TerraCycle is the name that comes up. The company has outposts in twenty-one countries and specializes in accepting the hard to recycle: lamps, aerosol cans, razors, candy wrappers, and much more. Its popular, if pricey, recycling programs include "Zero Waste" boxes that companies and individuals fill with particular items, such as bathroom detritus—old shower curtains, spent cleaning tools, and plastic packaging—and send back for processing. TerraCycle and its network sort and break down the waste into "building blocks" and then recycle the materials for new applications.

Lightbulbs

It takes extra steps to figure out what to do with expired bulbs. LED and CFL bulbs should be recycled for their glass and metal—not tossed, because the former have trace amounts of lead and arsenic, and the latter contain mercury. As for incandescent and halogen bulbs, it's generally recommended to dispose of these, wrapped, in the trash because their quantities of glass and metal are hard to recover. Check with your Department of Sanitation for special waste drop-off sites and disposal events, and consult the EPA's online list of places that recycle lightbulbs. Many Home Depot, IKEA, Lowe's, and True Value Hardware locations accept expired bulbs.

Mattresses

It's a nightmare scenario: some 18.2 million mattresses wind up in landfills in the US every year, each occupying 40 cubic feet (1.1 cubic meters) of space and taking hundreds of years to break down. Meanwhile, approximately 80 percent of mattress components can and ought to be mined for recycling: the fabric and fibers, wood, foam, plastic, and steel are all convertible into new products, such as carpet padding, insulation, mulch, and biofuel. Many municipalities offer scheduled mattress pickups—but only some are set up for recycling—earth911.com has a directory of mattress recycling plants.

MATTRESS RECYCLING COUNCIL
mattressrecyclingcouncil.org

With chapters in California, Connecticut, and Rhode Island, the Mattress Recycling Council provides a recycling plant locator plus information on potential recycling fees at its affiliate site, byebyemattress.com.

Medicine

According to the US National Library of Medicine, "thousands of tons" of medicine are released into nature each year, and "the scope of this potential problem is not to be underestimated." Don't dump—collect and drop off at the right locations.

DISPOSE MY MEDS
disposemymeds.org

This online resource lists independent US pharmacies that offer medication disposal.

DRUG ENFORCEMENT ADMINISTRATION (DEA)
deadiversion.usdoj.gov/drug_disposal/

The FDA recommends disposing of unused or expired medications at sites in your community that have

been authorized to collect and appropriately dispose of them by the DEA's Diversion Control Division. These include CVS, Walgreens, and other drugstores. The DEA lists Controlled Substance Public Disposal Locations on its site by zip code.

Paint

Keep your paint covered so it remains usable—and give away what you don't need through an organization like PaintCare (see below); schools, theater groups, and nonprofits are also good recipients, or post the paint on a neighborhood giveaway site. As a last resort, water-based paint is often accepted for curbside pickup. Oil-based paint, however, is considered hazardous waste—check to see if your sanitation department will take it or what's recommended. In both instances, it's best to fully dry out the paint (kitty litter can be used to expedite the process).

PAINTCARE
paintcare.org

A nonprofit run by the American Coatings Association, PaintCare partners with retailers to collect unwanted paint as well as primers, stains, and sealants. The majority get put back into use: Habitat for Humanity and Habitat ReStore locations, among others, are on the group's list of places where you can find their recycled-content paint.

PAY SOMEONE TO TAKE IT AWAY

When it comes to getting rid of stuff that no one wants and that you can't disperse yourself, begin by looking for local removal companies that focus on recycling, such as Donation Nation in the Washington, DC, area. Here are some nationwide options that say they donate and recycle whatever they can—talk to your local operator to make sure this is the case.

THE JUNKLUGGERS
junkluggers.com

Founded in 2004 with a single borrowed SUV, the Junkluggers now operate in twenty-nine states, and are reachable at 1-800-LUG-JUNK. Disposing of goods in the most responsible way is part of the Junkluggers' core mission.

LOADUP
goloadup.com

Something like Uber for junk removal, Load Up has a network of independently licensed and insured junk haulers in 49 states and 170 cities. Appointments are booked and tracked online.

Over our many months of working on this book, we noticed a heartening difference in the packing materials that came our way. In lieu of a nightmare mountain of plastic and Styrofoam, we started receiving simpler and far more planet-friendly options: repurposed cardboard, water-soluble packing peanuts, and even wooden crates filled with wood shavings and compostable honeycomb paper cushioning as protection instead of Bubble Wrap, all sealed with kraft-paper tape.

There are a lot of promising new plant-based packing materials emerging, including Green Cell Foam, a cornstarch-based replacement for polystyrene, and Mushroom Packaging, composed of mycelium and hemp shives. We saved the evidence, shown here, stored inside the largest of the crates, and have been putting it to reuse.

Glossary

Here's an elucidation of some words and expressions that come up in our book and/or get used frequently in discussions about the state of the planet and the earth-changing tasks that face us all.

AZO DYES: A group of synthetic colorants that accounts for 60 to 70 percent of the dyes used in the food, cosmetic, and textile industries. They are known for producing bright shades, but because of their deleterious effects on human and environmental health, there's a movement to switch to undyed and naturally dyed textiles and other products.

B CORPORATION: A label that helps consumers identify companies with a conscience. B Corp businesses have undergone a third-party certification process to ensure that they meet rigorous standards of social and environmental performance.

BIOACCUMULATION: When chemicals accumulate in the air and ocean, typically as a result of human activity, organisms take them in faster than they can get rid of them. Bioaccumulation implicates all steps of the food chain; for example, when we eat fish, we're often ingesting pollutants from a contaminated water source.

BIODEGRADABLE: A term used to describe a substance or object capable of breaking down into its natural elements. Technically, all substances are biodegradable over time, but glass, Styrofoam, and some plastics and metal can take hundreds of years to decompose into little pieces, which will never be fully incorporated back into the earth.

BIOPHILIC DESIGN: A design philosophy that aims to incorporate elements of the natural world into the built environment. Biophilic design is based on the concept that human health requires daily doses of nature—which can include direct exposure, via natural light and live plants, and indirect exposure, through natural colors and images of mountainscapes, for instance. (Shown opposite: With friends, Taryne Messer of Takata Nursery built herself a rooftop greenhouse in Brooklyn.)

CARBON FOOTPRINT: The total carbon emissions generated by a person or other entity, measured in tons of carbon dioxide per year. The tally comes from everyday activities: eating meat, driving a car, lighting a woodstove, traveling by plane, manufacturing and shipping goods, and so many more. The average carbon footprint of someone living in the US is about 16 tons per year, or four times the global average.

CARBON NEUTRAL: A blanket term for net-zero carbon dioxide emissions. A house, a business, even a country labeled "carbon neutral" has achieved a balance between carbon emitted and carbon saved. In construction, this is achieved via insulation, solar panels, and other energy-efficient designs. Dwellings that follow passive house standards often go beyond carbon neutrality by contributing excess energy to the power grid.

CARBON OFFSET: A monetary way to make up for carbon-producing activities. Purchasing one carbon offset represents the reduction of one metric ton of carbon dioxide in the atmosphere. The funds go toward an environmental project, such as a wind farm or solar energy field, that measurably reduces greenhouse gas emissions. Though seemingly a good thing, carbon offsets have worrisome ramifications: their popularity has enabled individuals and corporations to continue their destructive practices rather than change them.

CARBON SINK: Soil, plants, forests, bodies of water, and other (usually natural) elements sequester or capture carbon dioxide to use in photosynthesis. In doing so, they create "sinks" that lower the concentration of CO_2 in the atmosphere.

CIRCULAR DESIGN: In contrast to the long-standing production cycle in which goods are manufactured, used, and disposed of—a straight line to the garbage dump—circular design aims to create products out of existing materials, and to factor in their next incarnations as part of the design plan: old car tires, for instance, get used to make shoe soles, which later get turned into rubber roof tiles. Circular design takes into consideration "material banks"—construction castoffs and other salvage that are increasingly being shared via databases. See ellenmacarthurfoundation.org for an in-depth explanation of circularity.

CLEAN ENERGY: Clean energy comes from natural, renewable sources that do not have a harmful impact on the environment, such as solar, wind, geothermal, and hydro power. This is not to be confused with methane-emitting "natural gas" or "clean coal," terms promoted by petroleum lobbyists for refined but still horribly polluting versions of the fossil fuels.

CLOSED-LOOP PRODUCTION: A waste-free manufacturing approach in which materials are continually reused and recycled to generate new products (see "circular design" above). Aluminum cans are a good example: the metal can be continually recycled into new cans; the process of recycling the old ones and producing new ones requires energy and generates pollutants, but less than is required for creating new aluminum.

COMPOST: Decomposed organic material, often used to replenish soil and as a plant fertilizer, is known as compost (after the Latin *composita*, *compitum*, meaning "something put together"). To produce compost, organic materials must decay under the right conditions, including a warm temperature, nutrients, and oxygen. Household compost is commonly divided into two categories: green compost (think food scraps and grass clippings) and brown compost (dead plants, newspaper, cardboard). Some commercial products and packaging will safely decay in home compost without negatively impacting the compost's overall quality; these are known as compostables. Note that not all commercially compostable goods, such as plastic utensils made from corn-based PLA resin, will decay in a household composting setup. But many other things will: go to page 181 for a list of surprising compostables.

COMPOSTING TOILET: Toilets designed to convert human waste into usable compost date to the late nineteenth century. These models save water, reduce downstream pollution, produce fertilizer ("humanure"), and are convenient for off-grid setups without access to plumbing. Most composting toilets employ a system of multiple chambers with a bulking material like sawdust or coconut coir added to absorb liquid and promote airflow. For more, see the Green Building Alliance's report on composting toilets (go-gba.org/resources/green-building-methods/composting-toilets).

EMBODIED CARBON/EMBODIED ENERGY: The total carbon emissions associated with a building or product, embodied carbon considers all steps along the supply chain—from harvesting raw materials to transportation, installation, and disposal—in addition to active emissions. In the building sector, embodied carbon is responsible for almost a third of annual greenhouse gas emissions. Renovating or retrofitting existing buildings is one way to reduce the embodied energy of construction.

ENDOCRINE DISRUPTORS: A variety of common household products contain substances that interfere with the endocrine system by triggering the production or reduction of hormones, mimicking or transforming hormones, interfering with their signaling, or accumulating in hormone-producing organs. Common endocrine disruptors are BPA (in plastics), fire retardants (on furniture), and perfluorinated chemicals (in nonstick cookware). They've been linked to, among other things, disorders of the neurological and reproductive systems.

FIRE RETARDANTS: Starting in the 1970s, chlorine, bromine, and other chemicals were commonly applied to household products such as upholstered furniture, mattresses, and children's gear, with the intention of suppressing their flammability. In 2013, after these compounds had been linked to cancers, endocrine disruption, and fetal development abnormalities, the state of California led the way in banning them. But their use continues in many places, and they've also been shown to linger in household air and dust. When buying a mattress or any upholstered furniture, look for a label explaining that the item does not contain added flame-retardant chemicals. Go to the Green Science Policy Institute's sixclasses.org for more on why flame retardants are to be avoided.

GLOBAL WARMING POTENTIAL: Greenhouse gases trap heat in the atmosphere in differing amounts: methane, for example, absorbs twenty-five times as much heat as carbon dioxide, but the latter has a much longer-lasting effect. Global warming potential gives us a metric by which to compare the emissions associated with different activities and to reduce those that most contribute to global warming.

GRAY WATER: Household wastewater from sinks, showers, and washing machines that does not contain contaminants, such as human waste, is known as gray water (or greywater). To decrease overall water consumption, gray water can be repurposed, and is most commonly used to flush toilets, water indoor plants, and irrigate gardens. Recapturing gray water can be as simple as having a bucket in the shower to catch water wasted as it is heating up. More sophisticated reclamation systems include diversion, which routes gray water directly from the house to the yard—the easiest to install is a "laundry to landscape" setup best used for irrigating trees and bushes. Find information and online courses at greywateraction.org.

GREENHOUSE EFFECT: When heat radiating from the earth is trapped in the atmosphere by carbon dioxide and other greenhouse gases. Human activities, including deforestation and the burning of fossil fuels, are increasing this concentration, causing the planet's temperature to dangerously rise. The ramifications of global warming include extreme weather, wildfires, and drought.

GREENWASHING: The false billing of products as eco-friendly for marketing purposes, often through the use of unverified buzzwords like "sustainable," "green," and "biodegradable." To avoid falling prey to greenwashing, look for goods that are third-party validated by organizations like B Corporation and Cradle to Cradle (see page 226 for an overview).

HEAT ISLAND: The built world of roads and skyscrapers absorbs and emits heat from the sun and from manufactured things such as AC units, creating heat islands. These sweaty urban hotspots are in marked contrast to natural landscapes, where trees, plants, and bodies of water cool the air.

INDUCTION COOKTOPS: A flat glass cooking surface that uses electromagnetic energy to heat cookware directly. The latest models offer precise controls, fast cooking, easy cleaning, and energy efficiency—they use 10 percent less energy than even smooth-surface electric ranges—making them the environmentally friendly option of choice. Historically, induction ranges have been more expensive than gas and electric, but demand is helping to bring down prices. (See page 178 for more.)

KAPOK: A cotton-like fiber from the fruit of the kapok tree used in pillows, bedding, and more, as a plant alternative to down.

LEED CERTIFICATION: Short for Leadership in Energy and Environmental Design, LEED is the leading international rating system for environmentally friendly, cost-effective, energy-efficient residential and commercial buildings. On average, LEED buildings consume a quarter less energy and emit a third less greenhouse gases than uncertified buildings do. Since LEED was established in 1993, other ratings systems have emerged—WELL and Fitwel, for instance, focus on occupant health and well-being—but LEED remains the best known.

LIFE CYCLE ASSESSMENT: A methodology that measures the total environmental impact associated with a potential product. The stages along the supply chain are all factored in, including the energy required to extract raw materials and to distribute the finished goods. Businesses use life cycle assessments to comply with regulations and make more sustainable products.

MEDIUM-DENSITY FIBERBOARD (MDF): A building material made by mixing wood scraps with resin and wax and subjecting them to high temperatures and pressure to create a strong, dense wood product. MDF is a popular material for furniture and cabinet construction because it's affordable and lacks the knots and grain of real wood, making it easy to work with. Though produced from recycled materials, it has environmental drawbacks: a lot of energy is required in the manufacturing process, and hazardous chemicals like formaldehyde have traditionally been used as binders. Renewable base materials like straw and bamboo and nontoxic binders have the potential to make MDF more environmentally friendly. (See page 233 for more on composite wood.)

NET-ZERO HOUSE: A dwelling specifically designed to produce as much renewable energy as it consumes. These structures are extremely well insulated and have features like triple-glazed windows, state-of-the-art ventilation systems, solar panels, and gray water reclamation systems. See an example of an artful net-zero house on page 113.

OFF-GASSING: Think of the chemical scent that accompanies a fresh coat of paint, a new plastic shower curtain, even shampoo: that's the smell of volatile organic compounds and other chemicals being released into the air. Off-gassing most often occurs at indoor temperatures, and can lead to indoor pollution with a lot of health ramifications. Whenever possible, opt for products made from natural materials without additives.

OFF-GRID: Not connected to the electrical grid or other utilities. People living in off-grid dwellings often rely on solar panels and generators for power.

ORGANIC: Grown or produced without artificial chemical interventions. Certified organic materials such as cotton are grown with far fewer pesticides and fertilizers than conventional cotton, making them better for the soil, the farm communities involved in their production, and the consumer.

PASSIVE HOUSE: Built to a series of stringent specifications for ultra energy efficiency, passive houses can use up to 90 percent less energy than conventional dwellings. These structures are designed to minimize energy needs without sacrificing comfort, using strategies like airtight envelopes (which prevent heat loss in winter and cool air loss in summer, among other things), balanced ventilation systems, added layers of insulation, and high-performance windows to maintain steady indoor temperatures no matter the season. Go to page 307 to learn more from two architects who converted their historic town house to a passive house.

PASSIVE SOLAR: Passive solar design uses a building's siting and materials to capture natural energy: sun streams through strategically placed south-facing windows and is held in thermal masses such as stone and brick until nighttime, when it's dispersed to warm the house. "Although conceptually simple, a successful passive solar home requires that a number of details and variables come into balance," notes the US Department of Energy in its passive solar primer at energy.gov /energysaver/passive-solar-home-design.

RECYCLING: The process of diverting materials from a landfill, breaking them down, and using them again. Spinoff practices and terms include *downcycling*, or turning recycled materials into something of lower quality than the original due to the deterioration of its components, such as turning garments into automotive rags; *freecycling*, the practice of giving away rather than throwing away unwanted items (see a list of community giveaway networks, including freecycle.org, on page 324); and *upcycling*, using old materials to create a new product (a lamp made from a wine bottle; a quilt stitched from old cashmere sweaters), often of higher value than the original.

RED LIST CHEMICALS: Developed by the International Living Future Institute as part of its Living Building Challenge for more sustainable buildings, the Red List spotlights "worst in class" chemicals and elements—materials that pollute the environment, accumulate in the food chain, and harm human health. For a product or structure to be designated "Red List Free," its manufacturer or builder has to disclose all materials used and be found to contain none on the list.

REGENERATIVE DESIGN: Green roofs, wastewater treatment, and renewable energy production all fall under the future-minded approach known as regenerative design. Going beyond sustainability, which aims to use the minimum resources required, the regenerative approach aims to restore resources.

RENEWABLE ENERGY: A term frequently applied to wind, solar, and hydroelectric power, and other energy that comes from the earth and is not exhaustible. Labeling an energy source as "renewable," however, does not mean it's 100 percent green: hydroelectric dams, for example, can disrupt waterways and harm animal habitats.

RENEWABLE MATERIALS: Substances that come from living sources and can be replenished are considered renewable. Common examples include bamboo, cork, wood, and silk. (As opposed to nonrenewable materials like metals, natural stone, and plastic, which come from sources that have a finite supply.) Even renewable resources must be used carefully, however, as demand can easily outweigh supply.

RETROFIT: In building design, "retrofitting" refers to adding new systems to an existing older structure. In lieu of tearing down and starting afresh, retrofitting can be a cost-effective way to make dwellings more energy efficient. Techniques include the addition of insulation to walls, double- or triple-paned Low-E windows, and the installation of renewable energy systems like geothermal heat pumps and solar panels.

SICK BUILDING SYNDROME (SBS): A collection of symptoms, including headache, dizziness, nausea, and respiratory problems, that are common to a building's occupants. These conditions are often attributed to faults in the building's design, including poor ventilation systems and the presence of VOCs from paint, carpeting, and furniture.

STRUCTURAL INSULATED PANEL (SIP): SIPs are building materials used in place of traditional wall framing, and are manufactured off-site, thus streamlining the framing process. They can provide a high level of airtight insulation, which makes them especially critical in the building of passive homes. Most SIPs have petroleum-based foam insulation sandwiched between two boards, but it's increasingly possible to source bio-based insulation SIPs.

SUSTAINABLE MATERIALS: Substances that are abundant, natural, and renewable, and that can be produced without burdening the environment. Common examples include bamboo, hemp, linen, and straw.

THIRD-PARTY VERIFICATION: When a product is third-party verified, an independent auditor, known as a certification body, has reviewed and confirmed that it complies with a specified set of requirements. Third-party certification is the most reliable guarantee that a product does what it claims to (for more, see page 226).

VIRGIN MATERIALS: In contrast to recycled materials, virgin materials, such as metal ores and wood, are sourced directly from nature. Manufacturing products using these raw materials depletes natural resources and requires more energy than reusing existing materials.

VOLATILE ORGANIC COMPOUNDS (VOCS): Carbon-containing chemicals emitted as gases by certain materials, especially paints, cleaning supplies, and building materials. VOCs can be detrimental to human health: they have been linked to issues including eye, nose, and throat irritation; headaches; liver and kidney damage; and possibly cancer. According to the EPA, VOC concentration is two to five times higher indoors than outdoors. Choosing products that are low-VOC or VOC-free can mitigate this exposure.

ZERO-WASTE LIVING: A trash-free lifestyle pioneered by environmental activist Bea Johnson, author of the book *Zero Waste Home* and the website of the same name. The once fringe approach now has scores of devotees who bring their own containers to buy food from the bulk bins, make their own household and beauty products, compost a wide range of scraps, and say no to anything destined for the landfill. Zero waste is an exceptionally high standard that, as Johnson puts it, celebrates "life based on experiences instead of stuff."

Acknowledgments

As we were working on *The Low-Impact Home*, our subject matter became more urgent by the minute, and many hands contributed to the project. We are so grateful to everyone on our team at Remodelista, especially our sounding board and arbiter of aesthetics, editor in chief Julie Carlson, and CEO Josh Groves and style director Justine Hand, both of whom wore countless hats.

Our enormous thanks to the people who welcomed us into their homes (and allowed us to keep returning with still more questions); to our designer Jennifer Wagner for translating our vision so masterfully into a book; and to our principal photographer, Matthew Williams, for collaborating with us on not only this but also three previous volumes (this one during a pandemic). A royal salute to these other talented photographers whose work also appears here: Aya Brackett, Titus Chan, Sarah Elliott, Justine Hand, Ben Hosking, Oskar Proctor, and Yannic Schon and Susann Probst of *Krautkopf*; and to photo wizard Sjoerd Laneveld of Digisense. And, of course, to the champion crew at Artisan: publisher extraordinaire Lia Ronnen; our whip-smart editor, Bridget Monroe Itkin; art director Suet Chong; design manager Maggie Byrd; production editor Sibylle Kazeroid; and copy editor/vintage cocktail accessories expert Ivy McFadden.

These people pitched in with invaluable research, wisdom, and, in a few cases, hard labor: Oliver Agger, Glenn Ban of Glenn Ban Interiors, Marnie Campbell, Catherine Connolly of Merida, Lily Edgerton, Oliver Freundlich, Sandra Goldmark, Kate Green, Alexa Hotz, Hollister and Porter Hovey of Hovey Design, Bobby Johnston and Ruth Mandl of CO Adaptive, Maude McCole, Mattie Mead, Taryne Messer, Summer Rayne Oakes, Byron and Dexter Peart of Goodee, Barbara Peck, Katrina Rodabaugh, Jonsara Roth, Carrie Schei of Salt House Mercantile, David Tanis, Ruby Trudgen of the Modern House, Linh Truong of the Soap Dispensary, Shanta Tucker of Atelier Ten, and Corinna and Theresa Williams of Celsious.

Finding great-looking, low-impact household goods was made easier thanks to the following designers and retailers from whom we sourced key products: Alabama Chanin, Alder & Co., Ameico, Another Country, Ardent, Area, Armadillo, Auntie Oti, Bloomist, by Humankind, Coyuchi, Cultiver, Deborah Erhlich, deVOL, Domi, Echoview Fiber Mill, Elsie Green, Evangeline, Flotsam & Fork, Fog Linen, George & Willy, Harvest & Mill, Heaven In Earth, Helen Milan, Hook & Loom, Iris Hantverk, Jinen, Kalon, Kathryn Davey, Kept, Lostine, Maharam, Mark Lewis Interior Design, Merchant & Mills, Mjölk, Morihata, Naturepedic, Objects by Camilla Vest, PlantPaper, Pod, Proclamation Goods, Purl Soho, Retrouvius, Rough Linen, RW Guild, Saipua, Salter House, Smithy, Sonoma Wool Company, Sweet Bella USA, Terrain, the Citizenry, and the Primary Essentials.

Lastly, we thank our families: our partners, who good-naturedly endured our dinnertime discussions about the merits of heat pumps and induction stoves, and our children, whose futures were foremost in our minds as we worked on this book.

Photography Credits

Photographs by Matthew Williams except as noted below:

Edward Bishop and Jim Stephenson, courtesy of the Modern
    House: Page 47
Aya Brackett: Pages 86–93, 221
James Champion for Another Country: Page 232
Titus Chan: Pages 6, 124–139
Coyuchi: Page 234
Hallie Easley: Page 290
Sarah Elliot: Pages 214–217
Tom Fallon for Retrouvius: Page 310
Angela Fama: Page 210
Justine Hand: Pages 60–71, 185, 187, 197, 198, 200, 201, 205, 213,
    223, 242–273, 276, 278–289, 333; back cover
Heidi's Bridge (Erik Steinberg and Emily Hirsch): Page 182
Ben Hosking: Pages 112–123, 302
Krautkopf (Yannic Schon and Susann Probst): Pages 164–171, 305
Richard Lam: Page 238
Courtesy of Maharam: Page 236
Karen Pearson: Page 202
Oskar Proctor: Pages 46, 49–59
Greta Rybus: Page 293
Tala: Page 228
Melissa Walbridge for Remodelista: Page 230

Index

About the Authors

Margot Guralnick is a coauthor of *Remodelista: The Organized Home*, writer/producer of *Remodelista: A Manual for the Considered Home*, and a long-standing member of the Remodelista team. Now based in the Bronx, she grew up outside of Boston, and practices New England thriftiness as a way of life. She has been a vintage collector since childhood, and makes botanical art from fallen leaves and branches.

Fan Winston is a longtime magazine editor and the founding editor of the Organized Home, a companion website to Remodelista. She was thrilled to write a book with her fellow Remodelista team member that champions the same principles—a respect for nature, a distaste for wastefulness—her Chinese immigrant parents instilled in her. In addition to working on this project, she serves as a library board trustee in her town of Maplewood, New Jersey, where she's helping shepherd the construction of an all-electric, LEED-certified public library.

About the Contributors

Julie Carlson founded Remodelista with three friends in 2007, and has been its editor in chief from the start (see the dining table where it all began—and Julie's Brooklyn apartment—beginning on page 14). This is Remodelista's fifth book with Artisan.

Matthew Williams specializes in photographing architecture and interiors, and in taking portraits of people at home. He grew up in New Zealand, lives in Brooklyn, and shoots for publications and clients around the world.

Justine Hand is a photographer, stylist, DIYer, and Remodelista contributing editor based in Newton, Massachusetts. Justine's creations and images appear throughout the book, and that's her kitchen and pet rabbit, Bunzo, on the back cover.

Jennifer Wagner lives in New York's Hudson Valley, and is a creative director and graphic designer. Her long list of clients includes *Martha Stewart Living*, where she and Fan Winston worked together.

Front cover image: Passive house kitchen design by CO Adaptive
Back cover image: Clothes Horse laundry rack by deVOL; plant-dyed wool
socks by Kathryn Davey

Coauthors Margot Guralnick and Fan Winston
Remodelista editor in chief Julie Carlson
Remodelista publisher Josh Groves
Principal photographer Matthew Williams
Style director Justine Hand
Designer Jennifer Wagner
Reporter Barbara Peck
Researchers Lily Edgerton and Maud McCole

Library of Congress Cataloging-in-Publication Data

Names: Guralnick, Margot, author. | Winston, Fan, author.
Title: Remodelista : the low-impact home / Margot
    Guralnick & Fan Winston ; with the editors of Remodelista ; principal
    photography by Matthew Williams.
Description: New York : Artisan, [2022] | Includes index.
Identifiers: LCCN 2022010980 | ISBN 9781648290145
Subjects: LCSH: Interior decoration—Environmental aspects. |
    Gardening—Environmental aspects. | Sustainable living.
Classification: LCC NK2113 .G87 2022 | DDC 747—dc23/eng/20220411
LC record available at https://lccn.loc.gov/2022010980

Artisan books are available at special discounts when purchased in bulk for
premiums and sales promotions as well as for fund-raising or educational
use. Special editions or book excerpts also can be created to specification.
For details, contact the Special Sales Director at the address below, or
send an e-mail to specialmarkets@workman.com.

For speaking engagements, contact speakersbureau@workman.com.

Published by Artisan
A division of Workman Publishing Co., Inc.
225 Varick Street
New York, NY 10014-4381
artisanbooks.com
Artisan is a registered trademark of Workman Publishing Co., Inc.

Printed in China on responsibly sourced paper
First printing, August 2022

10 9 8 7 6 5 4 3 2 1